MY

MISSPENT

YOUTH

MY

MISSPENT

YOUTH

Essays by
MEGHAN DAUM

OPEN CITY BOOKS

Open City Books
225 Lafayette Street, Suite 1114
New York, NY 10012
www.opencity.org

Printed in the United States of America

10 9 8 7 6 5 4 3 2 1

Library of Congress Catalog Card Number: 00-109347
ISBN 1-890447-26-9

These essays have previously appeared in different form in the following publications: "On the Fringes of the Physical World" in *The New Yorker* and *Personals: Dreams and Nightmares from the Lives of 20 Young Writers*; "Publishing and Other Near-Death Experiences" in *The New York Times Book Review*; "My Misspent Youth" in *The New Yorker*; "Inside the Tube" in *Open City*; "According to the Women I'm Fairly Pretty" in *Nerve*; "American Shiksa" in *GQ*; "Music Is My Bag" in *Harper's*; "Variations on Grief" in *The Bellingham Review* and *The KGB Bar Reader*.

TABLE OF CONTENTS

FOREWORD

This book has a theme. It has, despite appearances to the contrary, a *point*, one which is made somewhere in each essay and, with any luck, emerges at the end of the book as a *subject*, albeit an elusive and abstract subject—nothing that will be turned into a major motion picture starring Julia Roberts, although I suppose there's always hope for a Wallace Shawn vehicle, a one-man, experimental meditation on the psychodynamics of e-mail, air travel, floor coverings, sex, death, and various other cultural anxieties that surrounded bourgeois, urban life at the very end of the twentieth century. I have been told repeatedly that stringing these concepts together would be a bad idea, that I should, instead, focus on a more coherent topic, such as spirituality, dating, "new media," women's gymnastics, or, as was suggested by a member of the New York publishing community who called me up one day with a surefire book idea—madness.

This book is not about any of those things. If anything, this book is about not knowing what things are about and trying to sort matters out by using one's personal experiences and observations as a tool. Recently I was going through my files and ran across some notes I'd taken during a conversation with a magazine editor about what I'd promised would be no less than an eight-thousand-word treatise on the sociopolitical impact of R.E.M. videos on those who were born between 1965 and 1978. The advice from the editor seemed, more than anything, to encapsulate what this book is about.

stay speaking from experience,

the word aesthetic is a turn-off,

idea that generation has been paralyzed by irony has been said, so argumnt [sic] must be couched in terms of own experiece [sic],

true that people define themselves according to trappings rather than actual things? is this new? maybe it's just you . . .

The reason I never managed to complete an eight-thousand-word treatise on the sociopolitical impact of R.E.M. videos on those who were born between 1965 and 1978 was that I could not get through one paragraph without using "aesthetic" at least five times. The word may be a turn-off, but I could never come up with any other way to describe the central conflict of my life and illustrate the condition that I feel most strongly affects the way we as humans go about the business of living our lives: our habit of expressing ourselves through the trappings of particular ideas rather than through the substance of those ideas. (Sexy topic! Let's green-light it.)

Those notes date back to a few years ago, when I was frequently asked by glossy print publications to write think pieces on matters concerning Generation X—why Generation X is afraid of sex, why Generation X doesn't go to Broadway plays, why certain members of Generation X undergo existential crises of such magnitude that they are driven to bungee jump from bridges in New Zealand. These requests come up less frequently these days, either because I proved myself incapable of succinctly tackling the subject or, more likely, because Generation X has aged beyond the target audience for Nike and Coke and there are fewer occasions around which to wrap over-generalizing articles filled with phrases like "More and more" and "We're living in a time of . . ."

Just to clarify things, the R.E.M. idea had to do with a particular ambiance in the pop culture that, in the early- to mid-1990s, was supposed to convey "realness." I called it "the R.E.M. aesthetic." But it's largely moot now, because this aura is no longer used to sell Nikes and Coke. Judging from the commercials during the last Super Bowl, the next generation is clearly operating under a new aesthetic, and I'll leave it to the next overreaching young writer to unpack the semiotics of Britney Spears or 'N Sync, which I can only pray are dated by the time anyone reads this.

As for the rest of the pieces in this book, none of which bear any direct relationship to R.E.M. or Generation X (that term will not appear again in these pages), they are all about the way intense life experiences take on the qualities of scenes from movies. They are about remoteness. They are about missing the point. They are about the fictional narratives that overpower the actual events, the cartoon personae that elbow the live figure out of the frame. They are about the romantic notions that screw up real life while we're not looking.

These pieces are not confessions. They're about me but they're also about a lot of other things, and a few of the stories I tell never even happened. I am not a person who keeps a journal. Instead, I'm inclined to catalog my experiences and turn them over in my head until some kind of theme emerges and I feel I can link the personal banalities to something larger and worth telling. This may be the reason I often have difficulty remembering events as they actually happened. No doubt it is a symptom of my aforementioned *point*, which concerns the tendency of contemporary human beings to live not actual lives but simulations of lives, loving not actual people but the general idea of those people, operating at several degrees of remove from what might be considered authentic if we weren't trying so hard to create authenticity through songs and clothes and advertisements and a million other agents of realness. In other words, this book is about a world ruled by accessories, about a citizenry that expresses its tastes, its politics, its dreams, and its heartbreaks via the trinkets on its shelves. But maybe that's just me.

On the Fringes of

the Physical World

It started in cold weather; fall was drifting away into an intolerable chill. I was on the tail end of twenty-six, living in New York City, and trying to support myself as a writer. One morning I logged on to my America Online account to find a message under the heading "is this the real meghan daum?" It came from someone with the screen name PFSlider. The body of the message consisted of five sentences, written entirely in lowercase letters, of perfectly turned flattery, something about PFSlider's admiration of some newspaper and magazine articles I had published over the last year and a half, something else about his resulting infatuation with me, and something about his being a sportswriter in California.

I was charmed for a moment or so, engaged for the thirty seconds that it took me to read the message and fashion a reply. Though it felt strange to be in the position of confirming that I was indeed "the real meghan daum," I managed to say, "Yes, it's me. Thank you for writing." I clicked the "Send Now" icon and shot my words into the void, where I forgot about PFSlider until the next day when I received another message, this one entitled "eureka." "wow, it is you," he wrote, still in lowercase. He chronicled the various conditions under which he'd read my few and far between articles: a boardwalk in Laguna Beach, the spring training pressroom for the baseball team he covered for a Los Angeles newspaper. He confessed to having a "crazy crush" on me. He referred to me as "princess daum." He said he wanted to propose marriage or at least have lunch with me during one of his two annual trips to New York. He managed to do all of this without sounding like a schmuck. As I read the note, I smiled the kind of smile one tries to suppress, the kind of smile that arises during a sappy movie one never even admits to seeing. The letter was outrageous and endearingly pathetic, possibly the practical joke of a friend trying to rouse me out of a temporary writer's block. But the kindness pouring forth from my computer screen was unprecedented and bizarrely exhilarating. I logged off and thought about it for a few hours before writing back to express how flattered and touched— this was probably the first time I had ever used the word "touched" in earnest—I was by his message.

I had received e-mail messages from strangers before, most of them kind and friendly and courteous—all of those qualities that generally get checked with the coats at the cocktail parties that comprise what the information age has now forced us to call the "three-dimensional world." I am always warmed by an unsolicited gesture of admiration or encouragement, amazed that anyone would bother, shocked that communication from a stranger could be fueled by anything other than an attempt to get a job or make what the professional world has come to call "a connection."

I am not what most people would call a "computer person." I have utterly no interest in chat rooms, news groups, or most Web sites. I derive a palpable thrill from sticking an actual letter in the U.S. mail. But e-mail, though at that time I generally only sent and received a few messages a week, proves a useful forum for my particular communication anxieties. I have a constant, low-grade fear of the telephone. I often call people with the intention of getting their answering machines. There is something about the live voice that has become startling, unnervingly organic, as volatile as incendiary talk radio. PFSlider and I tossed a few innocuous, smart-assed notes back and forth over the week following his first message. His name was Pete. He was twenty-nine and single. I revealed very little about myself, relying instead on the ironic commentary and forced witticisms that are the conceit of most e-mail messages. But I quickly developed an oblique affection for PFSlider. I was excited when there was a message from him, mildly depressed when there wasn't. After a few weeks, he gave me his phone number. I did not give him mine but he looked me up anyway and called me one Friday night. I was home. I picked up the phone. His voice was jarring yet not unpleasant. He held up more than his end of the conversation for an hour, and when he asked permission to call me again, I accepted as though we were in a previous century.

Pete, as I was forced to call him on the phone—I never could wrap my mind around his actual name, privately referring to him as PFSlider, "e-mail guy," or even "baseball boy"—began calling me two or three times a week. He asked if he could meet me in person and I said that would be okay. Christmas was a few weeks away and he would be returning east to see his family. From there, he would take the short flight to New York and have lunch with me. "It is my off-season mission to meet you," he said. "There will probably be a snowstorm," I said. "I'll take a team of sled dogs," he answered. We talked about our work and our families, about baseball and Bill Clinton and Howard Stern and sex, about his hatred for Los Angeles and how much he wanted a new job. Other times we would find each other logged on to America Online at the same time and type back and forth for hours. For me, this was far superior to the phone. Through typos and misspellings, he flirted maniacally. "I have an absurd crush on you," he said. "If I like you in person you must promise to marry me." I was coy and conceited, telling him to get a life, baiting him into complimenting me further, teasing him in a way I would never have dared in the real world or even on the phone. I would stay up until 3 A.M. typing with him, smiling at the screen, getting so giddy that I couldn't fall asleep. I was having difficulty recalling what I used to do at night. My phone was tied up for hours at a time. No one in the real world could reach me, and I didn't really care.

In off moments, I heard echoes of things I'd said just weeks earlier: "The Internet is destroying the world. Human communication will be rendered obsolete. We will all develop carpal tunnel syndrome and die." But curiously, the Internet, at least in the limited form in which I was using it, was having the opposite effect. My interaction with PFSlider was more human than much of what I experienced in the daylight realm of live beings. I was certainly putting more energy into the relationship than I had put into any before, giving him attention that was by definition undivided, relishing the safety of the distance by opting to be truthful rather than doling out the white lies that have become the staple of real life. The outside world—the place where I walked around on the concrete, avoiding people I didn't want to deal with, peppering the ground with half-truths, and applying my motto of "let the machine take it" to almost any scenario—was sliding into the periphery of my mind. I was a better person with PFSlider. I was someone I could live with.

This borrowed identity is, of course, the primary convention of Internet relationships. The false comfort of the cyberspace persona has been identified as one of the maladies of our time, another avenue for the remoteness that so famously plagues contemporary life. But the better person that I was to PFSlider was not a result of being a different person to him. It was simply that I was a desired person, the object of a blind man's gaze. I may not have known my suitor, but for the first time in my life, I knew the deal. I knew when I'd hear from him and how I'd hear from him. I knew he wanted me because he said he wanted me, because the distance and facelessness and lack of gravity of it all allowed him to be sweeter to me than most real-life people had ever managed. For the first time in my life, I was involved in a ritualized courtship. Never before had I realized how much that kind of structure was missing from my everyday life.

And so PFSlider became my everyday life. All the tangible stuff—the trees outside, my friends, the weather—fell away. I could physically feel my brain. My body did not exist. I had no skin, no hair, no bones; all desire had converted itself into a cerebral current that reached nothing but my frontal lobe. Lust was something not felt but thought. My brain was devouring all of my other organs and gaining speed with each swallow. There was no outdoors, the sky and wind were irrelevant. There was only the computer screen and the phone, my chair and maybe a glass of water. Pete started calling every day, sometimes twice, even three times. Most mornings I would wake up to find a message from PFSlider, composed in Pacific time while I slept in the wee hours. "I had a date last night," he wrote, "and I am not ashamed to say it was doomed from the start because I couldn't stop thinking about you." Then, a few days later, "If you stood before me now, I would plant the warmest kiss on your cheek that I could muster."

I fired back a message slapping his hand. "We must be careful where we tread," I said. This was true but not sincere. I wanted it, all of it. I wanted the deepest bow down before me. I wanted my ego not merely massaged but kneaded. I wanted unfettered affection, soul mating, true romance. In the weeks that had elapsed since I picked up "is this the real meghan daum?" the real me underwent some kind of meltdown, a systemic rejection of all the savvy and independence I had worn for years like a grown-up Girl Scout badge. Since graduating from college, I had spent three years in a serious relationship and two years in a state of neither looking for a boyfriend nor particularly avoiding one. I had had the requisite number of false starts and five-night stands, dates that I wasn't sure were dates, emphatically casual affairs that buckled under their own inertia even before dawn broke through the iron-guarded windows of stale, one-room city apartments. Even though I was heading into my late twenties, I was still a child, ignorant of dance steps or health insurance, a prisoner of credit-card debt and student loans and the nagging feeling that I didn't want anyone to find me until I had pulled myself into some semblance of an adult. I was a true believer in the urban dream—in years of struggle succumbing to brilliant success, in getting a break, in making it. Like most of my friends, I was selfish by design. To want was more virtuous than to need. I wanted someone to love me but I certainly didn't need it. I didn't want to be alone, but as long as I was, I had no choice but to wear my solitude as though it were haute couture. The worst sin imaginable was not cruelty or bitchiness or even professional failure but vulnerability. To admit to loneliness was to slap the face of progress. It was to betray the times in which we lived.

But PFSlider derailed me. He gave me all of what I'd never realized I wanted. He called not only when he said he would, but unexpectedly, just to say hello. His guard was not merely down but nonexistent. He let his phone bill grow to towering proportions. He thought about me all the time and admitted it. He talked about me with his friends and admitted it. He arranged his holiday schedule around our impending date. He managed to charm me with sports analogies. He courted and wooed and romanced me. He didn't hesitate. He was unblinking and unapologetic, all nerviness and balls to the wall. He wasn't cheap. He went out of his way. I'd never seen anything like it.

Of all the troubling details of this story, the one that bothers me the most is the way I slurped up his attention like some kind of dying animal. My addiction to PFSlider's messages indicated a monstrous narcissism. But it also revealed a subtler desire that I didn't fully understand at the time. My need to experience an old-fashioned kind of courtship was stronger than I had ever imagined. The epistolary quality of our relationship put our communication closer to the eighteenth century than the uncertain millennium. For the first time in my life, I was not involved in a protracted "hang out" that would lead to a quasi-romance. I was involved in a well-defined structure, a neat little space in which we were both safe to express the panic and intrigue of our mutual affection. Our interaction was refreshingly orderly, noble in its vigor, dignified despite its shamelessness. It was far removed from the randomness of real-life relationships. We had an intimacy that seemed custom-made for our strange, lonely times. It seemed custom-made for me.

The day of our date was frigid and sunny. Pete was sitting at the bar of the restaurant when I arrived. We shook hands. For a split second he leaned toward me with his chin as if to kiss me. He was shorter than I had imagined, though he was not short. He registered to me as neither handsome nor un-handsome. He had very nice hands. He wore a very nice shirt. We were seated at a very nice table. I scanned the restaurant for people I knew, saw no one and couldn't decide how I felt about that.

He talked and I heard nothing he said. He talked and talked and talked. I stared at his profile and tried to figure out if I liked him. He seemed to be saying nothing in particular, though it went on forever. Later we went to the Museum of Natural History and watched a science film about the physics of storms. We walked around looking for the dinosaurs and he talked so much that I wanted to cry. Outside, walking along Central Park West at dusk, through the leaves, past the horse-drawn carriages and yellow cabs and splendid lights of Manhattan at Christmas, he grabbed my hand to kiss me and I didn't let him. I felt as if my brain had been stuffed with cotton. Then, for some reason, I invited him back to my apartment, gave him a few beers, and finally let him kiss me on the lumpy futon in my bedroom. The radiator clanked. The phone rang and the machine picked up. A car alarm blared outside. A key turned in the door as one of my roommates came home. I had no sensation at all, only the dull déjà vu of being back in some college dorm room, making out in a generic fashion on an Indian throw rug while Cat Stevens' *Greatest Hits* played on the portable stereo. I wanted Pete out of my apartment. I wanted to hand him his coat, close the door behind him, and fight the ensuing emptiness by turning on the computer and taking comfort in PFSlider.

When Pete finally did leave, I sulked. The ax had fallen. He'd talked way too much. He was hyper. He hadn't let me talk, although I hadn't tried very hard. I berated myself from every angle, for not kissing him on Central Park West, for letting him kiss me at all, for not liking him, for wanting to like him more than I had wanted anything in such a long time. I was horrified by the realization that I had invested so heavily in a made-up character, a character in whose creation I'd had a greater hand than even Pete himself. How could I, a person so self-congratulatingly reasonable, have gotten sucked into a scenario that was more akin to a television talk show than the relatively full and sophisticated life I was so convinced I led? How could I have received a fan letter and allowed it to go this far? Then a huge bouquet of FTD flowers arrived from him. No one had ever sent me flowers before. I was sick with sadness. I hated either the world or myself, and probably both.

No one had ever forced me to forgive them before. But for some reason, I forgave Pete. I cut him more slack than I ever had anyone. I granted him an official pardon, excused his failure for not living up to PFSlider. Instead of blaming him, I blamed the Earth itself, the invasion of tangible things into the immaculate communication PFSlider and I had created. With its roommates and ringing phones and subzero temperatures, the physical world came barreling in with all the obstreperousness of a major weather system, and I ignored it. As human beings with actual flesh and hand gestures and Gap clothing, Pete and I were utterly incompatible, but I pretended otherwise. In the weeks that followed I pictured him and saw the image of a plane lifting off over an overcast city. PFSlider was otherworldly, more a concept than a person. His romance lay in the notion of flight, the physics of gravity defiance. So when he offered to send me a plane ticket to spend the weekend with him in Los Angeles, I took it as an extension of our blissful remoteness, a three-dimensional e-mail message lasting an entire weekend. I pretended it was a good idea.

The temperature on the runway at JFK was seven degrees Fahrenheit. We sat for three hours waiting for de-icing. Finally we took off over the frozen city, the DC-10 hurling itself against the wind. The ground below shrank into a drawing of itself. Laptop computers were plopped onto tray tables. The air recirculated and dried out my contact lenses. I watched movies without the sound and thought to myself that they were probably better that way. Something about the plastic interior of the fuselage and the plastic forks and the din of the air and the engines was soothing and strangely sexy, as fabricated and seductive as PFSlider. I thought about Pete and wondered if I could ever turn him into an actual human being, if I could ever even want to. I knew so many people in real life, people to whom I spoke face-to-face, people who made me laugh or made me frustrated or happy or bored. But I'd never given any of them as much as I'd given PFSlider. I'd never forgiven their spasms and their speeches, never tied up my phone for hours in order to talk to them. I'd never bestowed such senseless tenderness on anyone.

We descended into LAX. We hit the tarmac and the seat belt signs blinked off. I hadn't moved my body in eight hours, and now, I was walking through the tunnel to the gate, my clothes wrinkled, my hair matted, my hands shaking. When I saw Pete in the terminal, his face registered to me as blank and impossible to process as the first time I'd met him. He kissed me chastely. On the way out to the parking lot, he told me that he was being seriously considered for a job in New York. He was flying back there next week. If he got the job he'd be moving within the month. I looked at him in astonishment. Something silent and invisible seemed to fall on us. Outside, the wind was warm and the Avis and Hertz buses ambled alongside the curb of Terminal 5. The palm trees shook and the air seemed as heavy and earthly as Pete's hand, which held mine for a few seconds before dropping it to get his car keys out of his pocket. The leaves on the trees were unmanageably real. He stood before me, all flesh and preoccupation. The physical world had invaded our space. For this I could not forgive him.

Everything now was for the touching. Everything was buildings and bushes, parking meters and screen doors and sofas. Gone was the computer; the erotic darkness of the telephone; the clean, single dimension of Pete's voice at 1 A.M. It was nighttime, yet the combination of sight and sound was blinding. We went to a restaurant and ate outside on the sidewalk. We were strained for conversation. I tried not to care. We drove to his apartment and stood under the ceiling light not really looking at each other. Something was happening that we needed to snap out of. Any moment now, I thought. Any moment and we'll be all right. These moments were crowded with elements, with carpet fibers and direct light and the smells of everything that had a smell. They left marks as they passed. It was all wrong. Gravity was all there was.

For three days, we crawled along the ground and tried to pull ourselves up. We talked about things that I can no longer remember. We read the *Los Angeles Times* over breakfast. We drove north past Santa Barbara to tour the wine country. I stomped around in my clunky shoes and black leather jacket, a killer of ants and earthworms and any hope in our abilities to speak and be understood. Not until studying myself in the bathroom mirror of a highway rest stop did I fully realize the preposterousness of my uniform. I felt like the shot in a human shot put, an object that could not be lifted, something that secretly weighed more than the world itself. We ate an expensive dinner. We checked into a hotel and watched television. Pete talked at me and through me and past me. I tried to listen. I tried to talk. But I bored myself and irritated him. Our conversation was a needle that could not be threaded. Still, we played nice. We tried to care and pretended to keep trying long after we had given up. In the car on the way home, he told me I was cynical, and I didn't have the presence of mind to ask him just how many cynics he had met who would travel three thousand miles to see someone they barely knew. Just for a chance. Just because the depths of my hope exceeded the thickness of my leather jacket and the thickness of my skin. And at that moment, I released myself into the sharp knowledge that communication had once again eliminated itself as a possibility.

Pete drove me to the airport at 7 A.M. so I could make my eight o' clock flight home. He kissed me goodbye, another chaste peck I recognized from countless dinner parties and dud dates from real life. He said he'd call me in a few days when he got to New York for his job interview, which we had discussed only in passing and with no reference to the fact that New York was where I happened to live. I returned home to the frozen January. A few days later, he came to New York and we didn't see each other. He called me from the plane back to Los Angeles to tell me, through the static, that he had gotten the job. He was moving to my city.

PFSlider was dead. Pete had killed him. I had killed him. I'd killed my own persona too, the girl on the phone and online, the character created by some writer who'd captured him one morning long ago as he read the newspaper. There would be no meeting him in distant hotel lobbies during the baseball season. There would be no more phone calls or e-mail messages. In a single moment, Pete had completed his journey out of our mating dance and officially stepped into the regular world, the world that gnawed at me daily, the world that fed those five-night stands, the world where romance could not be sustained because we simply did not know how to do it. Here, we were all chitchat and leather jackets, bold proclaimers of all that we did not need. But what struck me most about this affair was the unpredictable nature of our demise. Unlike most cyber romances, which seem to come fully equipped with the inevitable set of misrepresentations and false expectations, PFSlider and I had played it fairly straight. Neither of us had lied. We'd done the best we could. We were dead from natural causes rather than virtual ones.

Within a two-week period after I returned from Los Angeles, at least seven people confessed to me the vagaries of their own e-mail affairs. This topic arose, unprompted, over the course of normal conversation. Four of these people had gotten on planes and met their correspondents, traveling from New Haven to Baltimore, New York to Montana, Texas to Virginia, and New York to Johannesburg. These were normal people, writers and lawyers and scientists, whom I knew from the real world. They were all smart, attractive, and more than a little sheepish about admitting just how deep they had been sucked in. Very few had met in chat rooms. Instead, the messages had started after chance meetings at parties and on planes; some, like me, had received notes in response to things they'd written online or elsewhere. Two of these people had fallen in love, the others chalked it up to a strange, uniquely postmodern experience. They all did things they would never do in the real world: they sent flowers, they took chances, they forgave. I heard most of these stories in the close confines of smoky bars and crowded restaurants, and we would all shake our heads in bewilderment as we told our tales, our eyes focused on some distant point that could never be reigned in to the surface of the Earth. Mostly it was the courtship ritual that had drawn us in. We had finally wooed and been wooed, given an old-fashioned structure through which to attempt the process of romance. E-mail had become an electronic epistle, a yearned-for rule book. The black and white of the type, the welcome respite from the distractions of smells and weather and other people, had, in effect, allowed us to be vulnerable and passionate enough to actually care about something. It allowed us to do what was necessary to experience love. It was not the Internet that contributed to our remote, fragmented lives. The problem was life itself.

The story of PFSlider still makes me sad. Not so much because we no longer have anything to do with one another, but because it forces me to grapple with all three dimensions of daily life with greater awareness than I used to. After it became clear that our relationship would never transcend the screen and the phone, after the painful realization that our face-to-face knowledge of each other had in fact permanently contaminated the screen and the phone, I hit the pavement again, went through the motions of real life, said "hello" and "goodbye" to people in the regular way. In darker moments, I remain mortified by everything that happened with PFSlider. It terrifies me to admit to a firsthand understanding of the way the heart and the ego are entwined. Like diseased trees that have folded in on one another, our need to worship fuses with our need to be worshipped. Love eventually becomes only about how much mystique can be maintained. It upsets me even more to see how this entanglement is made so much more intense, so unhampered and intoxicating, by way of a remote access like e-mail. But I'm also thankful that I was forced to unpack the raw truth of my need and stare at it for a while. This was a dare I wouldn't have taken in three dimensions.

The last time I saw Pete he was in New York, thousands of miles away from what had been his home and a million miles away from PFSlider. In a final gesture of decency, in what I later realized was the most ordinary kind of closure, he took me out to dinner. We talked about nothing. He paid the bill. He drove me home in his rental car, the smell and sound of which was as arbitrary and impersonal as what we now were to each other. Then he disappeared forever. He became part of the muddy earth, as unmysterious as anything located next door. I stood on my stoop and felt that familiar rush of indifference. Pete had joined the angry and exhausted living. He drifted into my chaos, and joined me down in reality where, even if we met on the street, we'd never see each other again, our faces obscured by the branches and bodies and falling debris that make up the ether of the physical world.

PUBLISHING AND OTHER

NEAR-DEATH EXPERIENCES

Why can't book publishing be the way it is in books? Where are those heady nights on Beekman Place, those working days on lower Fifth, those underpaid trust fund girls with the clacking Smith Coronas and the clicking low-heeled pumps from I. Miller? Where are Bennet Cerf's entrepreneurial seeds, Maxwell Perkins' worshipful authors, Mary McCarthy's well-read bedfellows? Where are the editorial assistants lunching frenetically at the Oyster Bar counter? Where are the pneumatic tubes running directly from Vassar and Smith to Viking and Scribners, sucking young English majors down their chambers and depositing them at chewed, wooden desks with tins of lemon drops in the top drawers and manuscripts towering over the "In" boxes? Alas, lament entry-levelers everywhere, the thirties are gone. So are the forties, fifties, sixties, and seventies for that matter.

There comes a time for every aspiring book publisher when she recognizes that her career, though inspired by Mary McCarthy's, will not resemble it. After a few weeks steeped in proposals for self-help books or unauthorized biographies of cable-access television stars, she realizes that there is no longer a May Day parade, *The Nation* is not a publication immediately accessible to twenty-two-year-old English majors seeking reviewer positions, two-bedroom apartments on Jane Street are out of the single girl's price range, and Webster Hall is no longer filled with the literati but with drag queens. There comes a point when she notices that although she studied Homer, Austen, and Melville, she will not be publishing them. There are a few hold-outs from the "literary" camp, to be sure (the assistant may find herself remarking on the fact that here, in the world of books, "literature" is considered a category as specific as "how to" or "occult") but there seems to be a disproportion- ate number of Oprah bios, guides to better sexual relationships, and Near-Death Experience books, slugged for those on the inside as N.D.E. "A new N.D.E. title," screams the publisher, dollar signs glowing in her contact lenses. "Isn't this to die for?" To the publisher, N.D.E. means big excitement and big bucks. To the assistant it can also stand for "not doing editing," or "not drinking enough."

I've had a number of different editorial assistant jobs. Some of these were on high floors of midtown office buildings, stale and plasticy smelling, the kinds of places where employees fight to assert their iden- tities by tacking Polaroids of boyfriends and cats on their cubicle walls. Others were sweet and arty, housed in the sort of loft-like office where the Mia Farrow character in a Woody Allen film always seems to work. Still another office was so mouse infested that I found myself not just tapping but actually stomping my feet underneath my desk for hours at a stretch; it seemed the moment I stopped, a rodent would make its way from the floor to an open desk drawer, wherein I would later fish around for a pen and instead discover something that made me actually weep in disgust and then yearn for a career in investment banking.

For the editorial assistant, every day is a new near-death experience. As if "going toward the light," we chase after what literature there is, try- ing, at least in the beginning, to discover the genius in the slush pile who's going to elevate us from entry-level minion to the up-and-comer with the brilliant eye. Our job entails pretty much what it sounds like: assisting editors. We open our editors' mail and log in the submissions. We keep track of flap copy and back-cover blurbs. We notice when a typo appears on a jacket mock-up—there's a fine line between *Prozac Nation* and *Prosaic Notion*. We request contracts, fill out invoices, and, mostly, answer the phone again and again. "Candy Whatzit's office," we say. "Jillian Dazzlewitz's line," and then, when our personal line rings with the promise of a friend on the other end or even an author whose manuscript is sufficiently unhot that *we might actually acquire it ourselves*, we answer obediently, with the name of the company, blurted unintelligibly because four other lines are on hold. As all editorial assistants know, it is not acceptable to pick up the phone and deliver a simple "hello." This is a trapping of the editorially privileged, of those with more than one linen blazer and their own offices with radiators upon which cardboard-mounted book jackets are gleamingly displayed. I spent quite a lot of time in my editorial assistant days dreaming about when I'd be able to answer with a "hello." I even experimented with it intermittently, pulling it out like a pair of torn jeans on casual Fridays. "Hello," I'd say, with faux nonchalance at 7:30 in the evening after everyone had left. This usually resulted in the person hanging up, or my mother's voice emerging on the other end, insisting that such lack of professionalism surely wasn't going to result in a promotion any time soon.

So it's all in the phone greeting, the banter with authors and agents, the art of raising the pitch of our voices when we call the accounting department to ask what happened to that check for the $100,000 advance because the "author is desperately poor and the agent is ballistic." (The truth is that we discovered the check request under a pile of magazines on our desk two months after we were supposed to process it.) But the voice will fix everything. It rises when we're covering up our clerical errors, drops to sultry depths when we're schmoozing or gossiping or ordering a decaf cap (with skim milk) from the deli around the corner. We're secretaries fully versed in Derrida, receptionists who have read Proust in French. This is a land of girls. There are always at least ten of "us" for every one of "him." We've got decent shoes. We've got B.A.s in English from fancy schools, expensive haircuts, expensive bags, and cheap everything else. We've got the studio apartment with the half-eaten one-hundred-calorie yogurt in the mini-fridge. We've got one message flashing on the answering machine (it's Mom again), bad TV reception, and a pile of manuscripts to read before bedtime. We've got an annual take-home of $18,000 before taxes if we're lucky, a $100 deductible on the health insurance, which is useful about one year into the job when we reach that milestone of entering therapy (inspired by the books we're working on), when we have to remind ourselves that getting out of bed every morning is mandatory rather than optional, when we realize that the phrase "there's a lot of writing involved" as it pertains to a job is subject to interpretation.

Like all legends, the glamour of publishing that we read about in McCarthy's *Intellectual Memoirs* or Mary Cantwell's *Manhattan, When I Was Young* is likely to be shattered somewhere around the first anniversary of assistantship. Though our heroines were no doubt just as burdened by this age-old indentured servitude as we are, there's something in the retelling, in the breezy we-can-laugh-about-it-now quality of such memoirs that today's editorial slaves find confusing. It's as if a sepia tint has been imposed onto a thoroughly fluorescent-lit world. Unlike our predecessors, we find ourselves spending considerably more lunch hours waiting in line at Ess-A-Bagel than sitting at the counter at the Oyster Bar. We realize that we're spending a significant amount of office time changing the fax paper, chasing down botched contracts, and writing flap copy for *Thin Thighs in Three Seconds* rather than inhabiting a publishing world like the one Dan Wakefield evoked in his memoir *New York in the Fifties*, where "the booze ran freely and the talk was always funny, sharp, knowing, dealing with what we cared about most—books, magazines, stories, the words and the people who wrote them."

To the dewy eye of the editorial assistant, there is something about this mythos—the stiff patent leathers tromping around Madison Square, the particular literary drunkenness that seemed obtainable only from the taps of the White Horse Tavern, where Dylan Thomas met the shot glass that killed him—that feels lost, abandoned in nostalgia's inevitable recycling bin. Instead, there are lunches eaten while hunched over a plastic container of tri-colored pasta salad from the Korean deli. There are hundreds of hours spent at the copy machine duplicating manuscripts, thousands of phone messages scrawled on carbon message pads, and a few attempts to raise our salaries to something resembling at least the annual tuition fee of the college we attended (not including the cost of books). Nonetheless we persevere, dreaming of the day when we'll become an assistant editor, and wondering how we'll survive the ensuing years until that fabled associate editor position is dangled before our eyes. If we make it this far without ditching the whole thing and going back to school for yet another graduate degree, we, too, could be the star editor responsible for the true story of Howard Stern's near-death experience. A savory thought, yet one that, like the devil, threatens to drag us down by the sharp lapels of our Burberry raincoats.

It's a good thing we don't own any. We can't afford them. Besides, they're not as timeless as they once were.

My Misspent Youth

Earlier this summer I was walking down West End Avenue in Manhattan and remembered, with a sadness that nearly knocked me off my feet, just why I came to New York seven years ago and just why I am now about to leave. Certain kinds of buildings seem almost too gorgeous to belong to the actual world, or at least the present-day world. Given the aluminum siding and brickface that proliferates throughout most of the United States, I'm always amazed that massive, ornate residences like 838 West End Avenue, with its yellow façade and black hieroglyphics, or 310 Riverside Drive, with its gargoyles and cornices, are still standing and receiving mail delivery and depositing kids in and out of the front doors like pretty much any domicile anywhere. When I was growing up in northern New Jersey, just twenty-five miles away from Manhattan, I had no concept that actual people could live in such places. My first inkling came when I was seventeen. I walked into an apartment on the Upper West Side of Manhattan and decided, within two minutes, what the controlling force of my life would be.

It was the summer of 1987, and I was in the process of learning how to drive a stick shift. My father is a composer and he allowed me to drive him to Manhattan in our Plymouth Horizon in order to drop off some lead sheets to a music copyist he worked with. The music copyist lived on West End Avenue and 104th Street, in a modest four-room apartment in a 1920s-era building. The moment the rickety elevator lurched onto the sixth floor and the copyist opened the door, life for me was never the same.

There was nothing particularly fancy about the place. It was a standard prewar with moldings around the ceilings and, most likely, porcelain hexagonal bathroom tiles that were coming loose. Although I'm not sure if there were faded Persian rugs on the floors and NPR humming from the speakers, it was just the sort of place for that. The music copyist and his wife had lived there for almost twenty years and although rent was the furthest thing from my mind at the time, I can now surmise, based on what they probably earned, that the apartment was rent controlled, perhaps $300 per month. It's now difficult to imagine a time when I didn't walk into someone's apartment and immediately start the income-to-rent ratio calculations. But on that summer night, standing in the living room of this apartment, looking down on the streets whose voluptuous, stony buildings formed the shore to the river that so famously keeps *here* safely away from *there*, my life was changed forever. I mean no melodrama in this. From that moment on, everything I did, every decision I made, every college applied to or not applied to, every job taken or not taken, was based on an unwavering determination to live in a prewar, oak-floored apartment, on or at least in the immediate vicinity of 104th Street and West End Avenue.

I've always been somebody who exerts a great deal of energy trying to get my realities to match my fantasies, even if the fantasies are made from materials that are no longer manufactured, even if some governmental agency has assessed my aspirations and pronounced them a health hazard. Lately, my New York fantasy has proven a little too retro for my own good. Though I did come to New York immediately after college and lived, believe it or not, within four blocks of 104th Street and West End Avenue, it wasn't until recently that I began to realize that I wasn't having quite as good a time here as I once did. I say this as someone who has had a very, very good time in New York. I say this also as someone who has enjoyed a good deal of professional success here, particularly considering that I am young and committed to a field that is notoriously low paying and unsteady. But low pay and unsteadiness never really bothered me all that much. I've historically been pretty good at getting by on what I have, especially if you apply the increasingly common definition of "getting by," which has more to do with keeping up appearances than keeping things under control. Like a social smoker whose supposedly endearing desire to emulate Marlene Dietrich has landed her in a cancer ward, I have recently woken up to the frightening fallout of my own romantic notions of life in the big city: I am completely over my head in debt. I have not made a life for myself in New York City. I have purchased a life for myself.

As I write this, I owe $7,791 to my Visa card. To be fair (to whom? Myself? Does fairness even come into play when one is trying to live a dream life?), much of those charges are from medical expenses, particularly bills from a series of dental procedures I needed last year. As a freelance person, I'm responsible for buying my own health insurance, which is $300 per month for basic coverage in New York State. That's far more than I can afford, so I don't have any. Although I try to pay the $339 per quarter charge to keep a hospitalization insurance policy that will cover me if some major disaster befalls, I am often late in paying it and it gets canceled. But lest this begin to sound like a rant about health care, I will say that medical expenses represent only a fraction of my troubles. I need to make an estimated quarterly tax payment next month of $5,400, which is going to be tough because I just recently paid back $3,000 to my boyfriend (now ex) who lent me money to pay last year's taxes, and I still owe $300 to the accountant who prepared the return. My checking account is overdrawn by $1,784. I have no savings, no investments, no pension fund, and no inheritance on the horizon. I have student loans from graduate school amounting to $60,000. I pay $448.83 per month on these loans, installments which cover less than the interest that's accruing on the loan; despite my payments, the $60,000 debt seems to actually be growing with each passing month.

It's tempting to go into a litany of all the things on which I do not spend money. I have no dependents, not even a cat or a fish. I do not have a car. I've owned the same four pairs of shoes for the past three years. Much of the clothing in my closet has been there since the early 1990s, the rare additions usually taking the form of a $16 shirt from Old Navy, a discounted dress from Loehmann's, or a Christmas sweater from my mother. At twenty-nine, it's only been for the last two years that I've lived without roommates. My rent, $1,055 a month for a four-hundred-square-foot apartment, is, as we say in New York City when describing the Holy Grail, below market. I do not own expensive stereo equipment, and even though I own a television I cannot bring myself to spend the $30 a month on cable, which, curiously, I've deemed an indulgence. With one exception, I have not spent money on overseas travel. All of this is true, just as it is true to say that there have been times when I haven't hesitated to buy things for my home—some rugs, a fax machine, a $200 antique lamp. There are even more times—every week, for instance—that I don't hesitate to spend money in a social capacity, $45 on dinner, $20 on drinks. I make long-distance phone calls almost daily with no thought to peak calling hours or dime-a-minute-rates. I have a compulsive need to have fresh-cut flowers in my apartment at all times, and I'll spend eight or ten dollars once or twice a week at the Korean market to keep that routine going. This behavior may be careless, but it is also somewhat beside the point. In the grand scheme of things, the consumer items themselves do not factor heavily; it's easier to feel guilt over spending $60 on a blender, as I did last month, than to examine the more elaborate reasons why I reached a point where I found it impossible to live within my means.

Once you're in this kind of debt, and by "kind" I'm talking less about numbers than about something having to do with form, with the brand of the debt, all those bills start not to matter anymore. If I allowed them to matter I would become so panicked that I wouldn't be able to work, which would only set me back further. I've also noticed that my kind of debt takes a form that many people find easier to swallow than, say, the kind of debt that reflects overt recklessness. I spent money on my education and my career. These are broad categories. There's room here for copious rationalizations and I'll make full use of them. I live in the most expensive city in the country because I have long believed, and had many people convinced, that my career was dependent upon it. I spend money on martinis and expensive dinners because, as is typical among my species of debtor, I tell myself that martinis and expensive dinners are the entire *point*—the point of being young, the point of living in New York City, the point of *living*. In this mind-set, the dollars spent, like the mechanics of a machine no one bothers to understand, become an abstraction, an intangible avenue toward self-expression, a mere vehicle of style.

I grew up in the kind of town that probably comes as close to defining a generalized notion of the American Dream as any. It's an affluent, New Jersey suburb whose main draw is its good public school system. As in many well-to-do suburbs, if you're not in need of K-12 services, there's not much in it for you, and so virtually no one between the ages of eighteen and thirty-five can afford or has reason to live there. The result is that the teenager is king. He sets the cultural and intellectual standard for the community. Moreover, he does so without the benefit of any adult influence other than his parents.

As I try to sort out the origins of my present financial situation, I always come back to the feelings I had as a teenager in the suburbs and the ineffable hankering I felt to access some kind of earthier, more "intellectual" lifestyle. When I was growing up in the 1980s, the cultural hegemony of my world was mired in a 1950s sensibility that came directly out of the parents' nostalgia about their youths. I went to parties in junior high school where we actually danced to *The Big Chill* sound-track. Kids wore Bermuda shorts and seersucker shirts. Unlike the self-conscious vibe of the world I entered later in college, there was nothing ironic in any of this. We knew no one older than ourselves or younger than our parents—no college or graduate students, no single profes-sionals, barely anyone who worked outside of a corporate structure. Therefore the teen agenda looked a lot like the parental agenda, which was, even though it was the late 1980s, pretty much an Eisenhower-era paradigm: college, work, marriage, return to suburbs. As adolescents we were, for better or worse, the staple crop and chief export of the place. Realtors have been known to drive prospective home buyers throughout the town and point out houses in which kids have gone to Ivy League colleges.

My family was in a unique situation because we lived off of my father's income as a freelance composer. Although I never had the sense that we were poor, I now realize that we must have, at certain times anyway, come pretty close to it. The main reason I never felt poor was that my parents, who had experienced their own kind of lifestyle epiphany when they were first exposed to academic settings, had an aesthetic value system that was less a reflection of having or not having money than with, in our opinion anyway, good taste. Unlike the neighbors, who had expensive wall-to-wall carpet and furniture sets from Seaman's, we had wood floors and oriental rugs, and I grew up believing that we were superior because of it. Even when I got older and began to run into my financial problems, I never had a conscious desire for a lot of money. I was never interested in being rich. I just wanted to live in a place with oak floors.

In what emerged as the major misconception of the subsequent twelve years, I somehow got the idea that oak floors were located exclusively in New York City. This came chiefly from watching Woody Allen movies. I wanted to live someplace that looked like Mia Farrow's apartment in *Hannah and Her Sisters* (little did I know that it *was* Mia Farrow's apartment). To me, this kind of space did not connote wealth. These were places where the paint was peeling and the rugs were frayed, places where smart people sat around drinking gin and tonics, having interesting conversations, and living, according to my logic, in an *authentic* way. As far as I was aware at seventeen, rich was something else entirely. Rich meant monstrous Tudor-style houses in the ritzy section of my town. Rich were the handful of kids who drove BMWs to school. I had the distinct feeling that my orthodontist, whose sprawling ranch house had front steps that were polished in such a way that they looked like they were made of ice, was rich. None of these particular trappings of wealth held my attention. In fact, nothing outside of the movies really held my attention until that night in 1987 when I saw the apartment on 104th Street.

How different the ride down that clanking elevator was from the ride up! Like a lover to whom you suddenly turn one morning and feel nothing but loathing, my relationship to my suburban town went, in the time it took that elevator to descend six floors, from indifference to abhorrence. With all the drama and preciousness of a seventeen-year-old girl, I now realized the pathetic smallness of my world. I now saw the suburbs, as I announced to my father, "for what they really are." The suburb/city alliance was, in my opinion, an unequal partnership between parasite and host, a dynamic permanently tainted by a sense that although the suburbs cannot live without the city, the city would hardly notice if the suburbs were all spontaneously irradiated by a tyrannical dictator of a distant star system.

Worst of all, the suburbs were a place from which escape held little romance. Unlike the kid from the small midwestern or southern town who saves up for bus money to come to the big town, the suburban New Jersey teenager who sits in her bedroom, listening to 1980s Suzanne Vega records and longing for some life that is being vaguely described in the songs—"my name is Luka, I live on the second floor" (could this be on 104th Street?)— doesn't elicit much sympathy. But I persevered, planning my escape through the standard channels: college selection. I'd seen the music copyist's apartment during the summer between my junior and senior years of high school and so applying to college that fall became a matter of picturing the apartment and wondering what kind of college an inhabitant of such an apartment would have attended.

My logic, informed by a combination of college guidebooks and the alma maters of those featured in the *New York Times* wedding announcements, went something like this: Bryn Mawr rather than Gettysburg, Columbia rather than N.Y.U., Wisconsin rather than Texas, Yale rather than Harvard, Vassar rather than Smith. My ranking system had nothing to do with the academic merits of the schools. It was more a game of degrees of separation from Upper West Side house plants and intellectualism. Somehow, Vassar emerged as the most direct route. After all, Meryl Streep, a girl from suburban New Jersey, had gone there (and later played Woody Allen's ex-wife in *Manhattan*), as well as the Apthorp-dwelling Rachel Samstadt in *Heartburn*, a character based on Nora Ephron, a personal role model of mine, not to mention a real life resident of The Apthorp. I also had some vague notions about getting myself into a position where I could become a writer, and this had something to do with being "artsy." So in a manner particular to restless suburban girls who consider themselves "different" and "unconventional" in much the same way that protagonists in young adult novels are portrayed, I was so consumed with going to a particular kind of artsy college and mixing with a particular kind of artsy crowd that I could do nothing during my entire senior year of high school but throw wads of paper into a wastebasket from across the room and say "If I make this shot, I get into Vassar."

I made the shot. I went to Vassar. It was either the best move of my life or the biggest mistake. I'm still not sure which. Though it would be five years until I entered my debt era, my years at Vassar did more than expand my intellect. They expanded my *sense of entitlement* so much that, by the end, I had no ability to separate myself from the many extremely wealthy people I encountered there. For the record, let me say that a large part of that sense of entitlement has been a very good thing for me. Self-entitlement is a quality that has gotten a bad name for itself and yet, in my opinion, it's one of the best things a student can get out of an education. Much of my success and happiness is a direct result of it. But self-entitlement has also contributed to my downfall, mostly because of my inability to recognize where ambition and chutzpah end and cold, hard cash begins. Like the naïve teenager who thought Mia Farrow's apartment represented the urban version of middle-class digs, I continued to believe throughout college that it wasn't fabulous wealth I was aspiring to, merely hipness.

Though there were lots of different kinds of kids at Vassar, I immediately found the ones who had grown up in Manhattan, and I learned most of what I felt I needed to know by socializing with them. In this way, my education was primarily about becoming fully versed in a certain set of references that, individually, have very little to do with either a canon of knowledge as defined by academia or preparation for the job market. My education had mostly to do with speaking the language of the culturally sophisticated, with having a mastery over a number of points of cultural trivia ranging from the techniques of Caravaggio to the discography of The Velvet Underground. This meant being privy to the kind of information that is only learned from hours spent hanging out with friends in dorm rooms and is therefore unavailable to those buried in the library trying to keep their scholarships or working at Stereo World trying to pay the bills. It is to have heard rumors that Domino's Pizza has ties to the pro-life movement, that Bob Dylan's mother invented White-Out and that Jamie Lee Curtis is a hermaphrodite. It is to never wear nude panty hose, never smoke menthol cigarettes, never refer to female friends as "girlfriends," and never listen to Billy Joel in earnest. It is to know at least two people featured in the *New*

York Times wedding pages on any given Sunday and to think nothing of putting $80 towards a bridal shower dinner at a chic restaurant for one of these people. It is to know that anyone who uses the word "chic" is anything but. It is to know arugula from iceberg lettuce, Calder from Klimt, Truffaut from Cassevetes. It is to be secure in one's ability to grasp these comparisons and weigh one against the other within a fraction of a second, to know, as my Jewish Manhattanite friends put it, "from stuff"—to know from real estate, from contemporary fiction, from clothing designers and editors of glossy magazines and Shakespearean tragedies and skirt lengths. Name-dropping was my drug of choice and I inhaled the stuff. By the time graduation came, I'd earned a degree in English, but that seemed incidental to my stellar achievements in the field of "from stuff."

I still wanted to be a writer. And with my ever-evolving sense of entitlement, that seemed more possible than ever. When I graduated in 1992, I followed a herd of my classmates into Manhattan, many of whom moved back in with their parents on Park Avenue. I got myself an entry-level job in publishing, and, along with a couple of friends, rented a five-room, prewar apartment with chipping paint on 100th Street and Riverside Drive, a mere four blocks from the scene of my 1987 epiphany. I was ecstatic. Such expert marksmanship! Such rich rewards for thorough research and careful planning. My job, as an editorial assistant at a glossy fashion magazine, paid $18,000 a year. The woman who hired me, herself a 1950s-era Vassar graduate, told me that she hoped I had an independent source of income, as I surely wouldn't be able to support myself on my salary. But I did support myself. My roommates, an elementary school teacher who was making $19,000 a year and a film student who worked part-time at a non-profit arts organization, supported themselves too. We each paid around $550 per month and lived as recent graduates should, eating ramen noodles and $.99 White Rose macaroni and cheese.

Looking back, I see those years as a cheap, happy time. It was a time at which a certain kind of poverty was appropriate; anything ritzier would have been embarrassing. Our neighborhood was a place for people who knew the city, for people *from* the city. Unlike the west seventies and eighties, which I've always experienced as slightly ephemeral, mall-like and populated by those who've come from elsewhere, the residents of this neighborhood seem to give off a feeling of being very deeply rooted into the ground. It's also a place that has absolutely no investment in fashion. No matter what the decade, there's an odd 1970s quality to the neighborhood. It's a place where you can still find people wearing corduroy blazers, a place that has always made me think of both the television show *Taxi* and the cover of Carole King's *Tapestry* album. Though I was living completely hand-to-mouth, I loved my neighborhood and looked forward to moving ahead in my career and one day being able to afford my own place in roughly an eight-block radius. From my position at the time, that seemed well within the range of feasibility. It was 1993, I was twenty-three, and I'd received a raise so that I was earning $21,000. I had no idea it was the closest I'd be to financial solvency for at least the next decade.

I'd been told I was lucky to get a job at a magazine—I had, after all, graduated into what was being called the worst job market in twenty years—and even though I had little interest in its subject matter, I didn't dare turn down the position. Within my first week on the job, I found myself immersed in a culture that was concerned entirely with money and celebrity. Socialites sat on the editorial board in order to give input on trends among the extremely wealthy. Editorial assistants who earned $18,000 managed to wear Prada, rent time-shares in the Hamptons, have regular facials, and pay thousands of dollars a year for gym memberships and personal trainers. Many of them lived in doorman buildings in the West Village or Upper East Side, for which their parents helped foot the bill.

This wasn't my scene. I felt as far away from my *Hannah and Her Sisters* fantasy as I had in the suburbs. I didn't want to be rich. I just wanted to live in New York and be a writer. Moreover, I wanted to be a writer in New York immediately. After a year of office work, I decided that an M.F.A. program in creative writing would provide the most direct route to literary legitimacy. I applied to exactly one program, Columbia, which, not coincidentally, happened to be located in my neighborhood. It's also the most expensive writing program in the country, a fact I ignored because the students, for the most part, seemed so down-to-earth and modest. Unlike my Prada-wearing, Hamptons-going colleagues from the magazine, Columbia students, in their flannel shirts and roach-infested student housing, seemed as earnest and unrich as I was, and I figured that if they could take out $20,000-a-year loans, so could I. Even as I stayed at Columbia for three years and borrowed more than $60,000 to get my degree, I was told repeatedly, by fellow students, faculty, administrators, and professional writers whose careers I wished to emulate, not to think about the loans. Student loans, after all, were low interest, long term, and far more benign than credit-card debt. Not thinking about them was a skill I quickly developed.

If there is a line of demarcation in this story, a single moment where I crossed the boundary between debtlessness and total financial mayhem, it's the first dollar that I put toward achieving a life that had less to do with overt wealth than with what I perceived as intellectual New York bohemianism. It seems laughable now, but at the time I thought I was taking a step down from the Chanel suits and Manolo Blahniks of my office job. Hanging out at the Cuban coffee shop and traipsing over the syringes and windblown trash of upper Broadway, I was under the impression that I was, in a certain way, slumming. And even though I was having a great time and becoming a better writer, the truth was that the year I entered graduate school was the year I stopped making decisions that were appropriate for my situation and began making a rich person's decisions. Entering this particular graduate program was a rich person's decision. But it's hard to recognize that you're acting like a rich person when you're becoming increasingly poor. Besides, I was never without a job. I worked for an anthropology professor for $9 an hour. I read manuscripts at $10 a pop for a quack literary agent. I worked at a university press for $10 an hour. Sometimes I called in sick to these jobs and did temp work in midtown offices for $17 an hour. A couple of times I took out cash advances on my credit cards to pay the rent.

There were a handful of us who were pulling these kinds of stunts. My roommate had maxed out her credit cards in order to finance a student film. I knew several women and even a few men who were actively looking for rich marriage partners to bail them out of their debt. One aspiring novelist I know underwent a series of drug treatments and uncomfortable surgical procedures in order to sell her eggs for $2,500. A couple of promising writers dropped out of the program and left the city. These days, when I talk to the people who left, they give off the sense of having averted a car crash but by the same token, they wonder if they'd be farther along in their careers had they stuck it out. But this question of sticking it out has less to do with M.F.A. programs than with the city in general. Whether or not one is paying $20,000 a year to try to make it as a writer, New York City has become a prohibitively expensive place to live for just about anyone. Although I've devoted a lot of energy to being envious of Columbia classmates whose relatives were picking up the tab for their educations, it's now becoming clear to me that assuming the presence of a personal underwriter is not limited to entry-level jobs at glossy magazines or expensive graduate programs. These days, being a creative person in New York is, in many cases, contingent upon inheriting the means to do it.

But the striver in me never flinched. As I was finishing at Columbia, my writing career was giving off signs that it might actually go somewhere. If I hadn't been doing so well I might have pulled out of the game. I would have gotten a job, started paying my bills, and averted my own impending car crash. Instead, I continued to hedge my bets. I was publishing magazine articles regularly and, after a few months of temping at insurance companies and banks, scored some steady writing gigs that, to my delight, allowed me to work as a full-time freelance writer. After five years and eight different roommates in the 100th Street apartment, I was earning enough money to move to my own place and, more importantly, had garnered enough contacts with established Manhattanites to find myself a two-year sublet in a rent-stabilized apartment. The fact that I got this sublet through a connection from a Columbia professor has always struck me as justification enough for the money I spent to go to school; as we all know by now, the value of a rent-stabilized one-bedroom is equal to if not greater than that of a master's degree or even the sale of a manuscript to a publisher. And though I still had not hit the literary jackpot by producing the best-seller that would pay off my loans and buy me some permanent housing, I still felt I'd come out ahead in the deal.

So it's not that I was sold a complete bill of goods. Things were going well. In 1997 I was twenty-seven, teaching a writing course at N.Y.U., publishing in a variety of national magazines, and earning about $40,000 a year after taxes. (The teaching job, incidentally, paid a paltry $2,500 for an entire semester but I was too enamored with the idea of being a college teacher to wonder if I could afford to take it.) Neither clueless suburbanite nor corporate, subsidized yuppie, I could finally begin practicing the life I'd spent so long studying for. I had a decent-sized apartment with oak floors and porcelain hexagonal bathroom tiles that were coming loose. Like an honest New Yorker, I even had mice lurking in the kitchen. I bought the rugs and the fax machine. I installed a second telephone line for fax/data purposes.

Soon, however, I had some hefty dental bills that I was forced to charge to Visa. I tried not to think about that too much until I ended up making a few doctor's visits that, being uninsured, I also charged to Visa. When April rolled around, I realized my income was significantly higher that year than any previous year and that I had woefully under-estimated what I owed the IRS. Despite a bevy of the typical free-lancer's write-offs—haircuts, contact lenses, an $89.99 sonic rodent control device—I was hit with a tax bill of over $20,000. And although the IRS apparently deemed sonic rodent control devices an acceptable deduction, it seemed that I'd earned too much money to be eligible to write off the nearly $7,000 (most of it interest) I'd paid to the student loan agency or the $3,000 in dental bills. Most heartbreaking of all, my accountant proffered some reason that my $60 pledge to WNYC—my Upper West Side tableau couldn't possibly be complete without the NPR coffee mug—was not tax deductible as advertised. In the months it took me to assemble that $20,000 I had to reduce my monthly student loan payments from the suggested $800 per month to the aforementioned $448.83 per month, a reduction that effectively ensured that I wouldn't touch the principal for years. I continued to pay my $1,055 per month rent, and made every effort to pay the phone, gas, and electric bills, the American Express bills, and the hospitalization-only medical coverage.

It was around this time that I started having trouble thinking about anything other than how to make a payment on whatever bill was sitting on my desk, most likely weeks overdue, at any given time. I started getting collection calls from Visa, final disconnection notices from the phone company, letters from the gas company saying "Have you forgotten us?" I noticed that I was drinking more than I had in the past, often alone at home where I would sip Sauvignon Blanc at my desk and pretend to write when in fact I'd be working out some kind of desperate math equation on the toolbar calculator, making wild guesses as to when I'd receive some random $800 check from some unreliable accounting department of some slow-paying publication, how long it would take the money to clear into my account, what would be left after I set aside a third of it for taxes and, finally, which lucky creditor would be the recipient of the cash award. There's nothing like completing one of these calculations, realizing that you've drunk half a bottle of $7.99 wine, and feeling more guilt about having spent $7.99 than the fact that you're now too tipsy to work. One night I did a whole bunch of calculations and realized that despite having earned a taxable income of $59,000 in 1998, despite having not gone overboard on classic debtor's paraphernalia like clothes and vacations and stereo equipment, despite having followed the urban striver's guide to success, I was more than $75,000 in the hole.

There are days when my debt seems to be at the center of my being, a cancer that must be treated with the morphine of excuses and rationales and promises to myself that I'm going to come up with the big score—book advance, screenplay deal, Publisher's Clearing House prize—and save myself. There are other days when the debt feels like someone else's cancer, a tragedy outside of myself, a condemned building next door that I try to avoid walking past. I suppose that's why I'm even able to publicly disclose this information. For me, money has always, truly, been "only money," a petty concern of the shallower classes, a fatuous substitute for more important things like fresh flowers and "meaningful conversations" in the living room. But the days when I can ignore the whole matter are growing further and further apart. My rent-stabilized sublet is about to expire, and I now must find somewhere else to live. I have friends getting rich off the stock market and buying million-dollar houses. I have other friends who are almost as bad off as I am and who compulsively volunteer for relief work in Third World countries as a way of forgetting that they can't quite afford to live in the first world.

But New York City, which has a way of making you feel like you're in the Third World just seconds after you've thought you conquered all of western civilization, has never really been part of the rest of the world. In that sense, I suppose it's foolish to believe that one can seek one's fortune, or at least one's sustenance, through rational means. I suppose that part of the city's magical beastliness is the fact that you can show up with the best of intentions, do what's considered to be all the right things, actually achieve some measure of success and still find yourself caught inside a financial emergency.

I have to be out of my sublet by September 1. Even if I tried to assume control of the lease, the landlord will renovate the apartment and raise the rent to $2,000. I told a friend about this the other day, hoping she would gasp or give me some sort of reaction. Instead she said, "That's cheaper than our place." A two-bedroom apartment down the street rented for $4,500 a month. A studio anywhere in Manhattan or the "desirable" parts of Brooklyn will go for an average of $1,750. West 104th Street is totally beyond my means. Worse, 104th Street is now beyond the means of most of the people that made me want to live there in the first place. The New York that changed my life on that summer night when I was seventeen simply no longer exists.

Now, having taken all of this apart, I am determined to not put it back together the same way. Several months ago, on a day when the debt anxiety had flared up even more than usual, I arrived at the idea of moving to Lincoln, Nebraska. I'd been to Lincoln on a magazine assignment twice before, met some nice people, and found myself liking it enough to entertain the notion of moving there. But both times I'd discarded the idea of moving there the minute the wheels hit the tarmac at LaGuardia. Surely I'd never be able to live without twenty-four-hour take-out food and glitzy Russian martini bars. On this latest round of panic, however, I chewed on the idea for a while, decided that it was a good plan, and have pretty much continued to feel that way ever since. I can rent an apartment there for $300 a month. I can rent an entire house, if I want one, for $700. Full coverage health insurance will cost me $66 a month. Apparently, people in Nebraska also listen to NPR, and there are even places to live in Lincoln that have oak floors. Had I known that before, I might have skipped out on this New York thing altogether and spared myself the financial and psychological ordeal. But I'm kind of glad I didn't know because I'm someone who has had a very, very good time here. I'm just leaving the party before the cops break it up.

CARPET IS MUNGERS

Once, when I was desperately searching for an affordable apartment in New York City, I looked at a place that was gigantic by local standards. It had two bedrooms, a kitchen nook, a dishwasher, and a sweeping view of the East River. The building was staffed by twenty-four-hour doormen and had a running track and a garden on the roof. It rented for $400 a month. This was in a rental market where studio apartments rarely went for less than $1,100 a month, and it was unheard of to have sunlight let alone things like dishwashers and running tracks. I was in dire need of a place to live. I had precisely ten days to find something before I'd be forced to put my stuff in storage and sleep on a friend's couch. But I did not rent the apartment. I did not for one minute entertain the possibility of living there. I did not even look in the closets, of which there were many. The reason is that the apartment had wall-to-wall carpet.

Carpet makes me want to kill myself. Wall-to-wall carpet anywhere other than offices, airplanes, and Holiday Inn lobbies sends me careening toward a kind of despair that can only be described as the feeling that might be experienced by a person who has made some monumental and irreversible life decision and realized, almost immediately after the fact, that it was an error of epic proportions. Carpet makes me feel the way the woman who married the multimillionaire stranger on national television must have felt when she was on the plane to the honeymoon in Maui, the $35,000 rock on her finger, and her possibly sociopathic husband next to her in first class. Carpet makes me feel the way I felt when I was twelve and "went out" with Stephen Mungers, a boy from homeroom who I barely knew, for a week. In seventh grade, "going out" signified nothing more than a mutual agreement that the term would be applied to the parties involved; no physical contact or verbal exchange other than "You wanna go out?" and "Okay" was required. And even though the situation was entirely reversible, I remember that week as an unprecedented and traumatic psychological jaunt into a self that was not my own. I had, in the context of seventh grade and the various ideas I'd developed about who I was, become "other" to my own self. I felt somehow that I had betrayed a basic premise of my existence. And although I was unsure exactly what that premise was, I specifically recall spending that week practicing the oboe with such concentration and nervous energy that I finally mastered a particularly arduous exercise and decided, with more certainty than has since accompanied more serious matters, that as long as I went out with Stephen Mungers I would be wholly incapable of being the person I should be and, in fact, was. A similar effect occurs when I walk into a house where not one square inch of floor is showing.

Carpet is Mungers. Carpet is otherness. It is not my house and not the house of ninety percent of the people I know. It's more than just not my style, it's not my oeuvre. People always say to me, "Oh, I don't like carpet either. It makes me sneeze and it's so hard to clean." Sneezing and cleaning have nothing to do with my feelings on the subject. If *not* having carpet caused allergies and presented maintenance difficulties, I would tough it out. It's really shallow, I know. But I'm capable of being extremely shallow, far more superficial that I'm often given credit for. There's a lot of stuff I can look past—unemployed boyfriends, border-line personalities, offensive comments aimed directly at me—but when I balk, I balk hard. When you get to a certain age you learn what the deal breakers are.

But let's cut to the chase. Carpet is a class issue. I didn't make it that way, I'm just pointing it out. And I'm not talking about socioeconomic class. Carpet has, since its inception, been the province of the elite. It's found in high-rise condos and suburban ranch houses. Cheap landlords like to install cheap carpet in cheap rentals so they can raise the price—and it amazes and depresses me that people actually buy into this. But I also realize that many of the people who don't mind or even like carpet possess the kind of "class" that, in my earlier days, I believed ran in inverse proportion to wall-to-wall floor covering of any kind. In other words, I did not believe that they read books, owned classical music CDs, or were not necessarily members of the John Birch Society.

That false perception was the result of confusing "having class" with "having to have class." The kind of class that I associate with wood floors is the kind of class that emerges out of an anxiety about being classy. People who must have wood floors are people who need to convey the message that they're quite possibly better than most people. They're people who leave *The New York Review of Books* on the coffee table but keep *People* in the bedroom. They're people who say "I don't need to read *Time* or *Newsweek* because I can get everything I need from the *Times*." They're people who would no sooner put the television set in the living room than hang their underwear to dry on the front porch. They buy whole-bean coffee and grind it in a Braun grinder. They listen to

NPR, tell other people what they heard on it, and are amazed when the other people say they heard it too.

I am one of those people. My TV is in a room that also contains a pile of magazines I won't admit to reading, a Kenny Loggins CD I don't want anyone to see, and a Restoration Hardware catalog from which I want very much to order a Teacher's College Chrome Plate Schoolhouse light, if only Restoration Hardware was not so wannabe, so postiche. My apartment has oak floors and oriental rugs and, for as long as I can remember, oak floors and oriental rugs have played as great a role in my sense of well-being as the knowledge that after falling asleep I would eventually wake up. I haven't bought a can of Maxwell House in over ten years. I have an intellectual crush on former *Talk Of The Nation* host Ray Suarez and a WNYC coffee mug out of which I eat Grape-Nuts but never Total. I use Arm & Hammer laundry powder. The thought of owning a bed that is not a platform bed, i.e. one that has a box spring and therefore requires a dust ruffle, lowers my seratonin level. I do not wear colors any brighter than pale blue or dusty rose. I do not wear panty hose, only tights. I do not wear gold jewelry. I would never drive an American car. I stick to these rules because I am terrified of what would happen if I deviated from them. I fear the "other." I fear carpet.

Maxwell House is carpet. Total is carpet. All-temperature Cheer is carpet, as is commercial talk radio, dust ruffles, bright-colored clothing, pantyhose, gold jewelry, and the United States Automotive Industry. Carpet is the road you congratulate yourself for never having taken. Carpet is the woman at the supermarket whom you are glad not to be. Carpet is the house who bought the oddly-named and aggressively bland-tasting Savannahs when you sold Girl Scout cookies. Carpet is the job you held immediately after graduation, before you realized that a career in marketing posed a severe threat to your emotional health. Carpet is the distant relatives you see only at funerals. Carpet is the high school sweetheart you would have disastrously married had you been born one generation earlier.

Here is a brief, heartbreaking story about carpet. I once loved a great man. He treated me with that rare combination of adoration and decency best known to characters that were once played by Jimmy Stewart and are now played by Kevin Costner. He showed up at my door with flowers. He embarrassed me in front of the mailman by sending me letters addressed "To My Sweetie" on the envelope. He could have been the one were it not for the sad fact that he could never, ever have been the one. For a brief period during our two-year relationship, I fantasized about our wedding: a Wyeth-esque outdoor affair, tents and mosquito netting, and a string quartet playing Bach in a wheat field. I would wear a 1920s-era lace dress with a dropped waist and go barefoot. Friends would toast scintillatingly. *The New York Times* would run a Vows column with a headline like "Passion on the Plains." But such an event would never come to pass. He was, despite his old-fashioned ways and gentlemanly demeanor, a reception hall and DJ type of man. He listened to Yanni. He enjoyed the television show *Wings*. His house had carpet and he was not bothered by it. He had, in fact, paid to have it installed. Though I believe to this day that his soul, at its core, is as pure and as capable of embracing my required snobberies as is the soul of any man with oak floors, it was shrouded in carpet. It was suffocating in pale-blue shag and our love was eventually subsumed under an expanse of Scotch-guarded fibers.

Carpet is the near miss, the ever-present land mine, the disaster that looms on the horizon. It's the efficiency apartment you'll be forced to move into if the business fails, the marriage collapses, the checks stop coming in, and the wolf breaks down the door and scratches up those precious polished floors. Carpet can be there when you least expect it; some of your best friends could have it. It could be the bad news at the end of the third date; sprawling across the bachelor pad from wall to wall, it's what makes you decide not to go past first base. When I take a risk, what I put on the line are my essential, uncarpeted conditions. To venture into the unknown is to hazard a brush with the carpeted masses. They taunt and threaten from the sides of the road, their split-levels and satellite dishes forming pockmarks on the prairie, their luxury condo units driving up the cost of living.

Where there's carpet, there's been a mistake. Where there's carpet, there's Mungers. The arrangement is temporary. The clock is ticking. Carpet is a rental car, a borrowed jacket you'd never buy for yourself, the neighbor's key ring, with some tacky trinket attached, that you keep in case she locks herself out. Carpet makes everybody a stranger. Carpet tells me it's time to pack up and move on. When there's carpet, every street gets me lost. Every restaurant is a Denny's. Every room is a hotel room. My feet can't quite touch the floor. I am so far away from home.

INSIDE THE TUBE

They gather in small, blonde clusters at the gate, sipping coffee from the Terminal C Nathan's Famous, their clean hair swept carefully out of their clean faces. They cannot possibly be real, these uniformed creatures, these girls with matching luggage and matching shoes, these warm-blooded extensions of that hulking, spotless aircraft.

Neither passenger nor pilot, the flight attendant is the liaison between the customer and the machine. She is somehow blonde even when she's not blonde, a girl even when she's a guy. Part bimbo and part Red Cross, she is charged with the nearly impossible task of calming the passenger down while evoking enough titillation to suggest that there remains, even in the twenty-first century, something special about air travel.

Flight attendants are fetishized and mocked in equal measure. They are both fantasy and punch line, the players in hackneyed sex jokes and the guides through smoke and fire to the emergency exit. Since the beginning of commercial flying, back in the 1930s when flight attendants were required to be registered nurses, the profession has symbolized an unearthly female glamour. Until the 1960s, flight attendants were not allowed to be married. On many airlines they were required to have a college degree and speak a foreign language. Their skin was periodically checked for blemishes, their hair was not allowed to touch their collars, and if they were, say, 5'4", they could not weigh more than 115 pounds. Until the 1970s they were called "stewardesses," real girls who were treated like ladies.

There is no small amount of perverted nostalgia in all of this. When people today talk about what's happened to flying, about why any given transcontinental flight bears a heavy resemblance to a Greyhound bus ride from Memphis to Louisville, they often claim to be talking largely about the absence of ethereal waitresses serving seven-course meals in first class. No longer does the starchy hiss of the uniform sound a note of almost military kinkiness. Back in the old days, flight attendants were as sleek and identical as F-16s flying in formation. Back in the old days, they may as well have all been twin sisters. There was a time when you could pinch their asses and they'd buy you a martini. These days they will stop serving you drinks when you've had enough. If you do anything that they feel interferes with their duties, you could be charged with a felony. There are restraints in the cockpit should such an occasion arise. These days you have your fat ones, your ugly ones, and worst of all, your old ones. It used to be they had to quit when they turned thirty. Today, with no retirement age, there are a few as old as seventy-seven.

But even now, perhaps even this morning when you boarded some generic flight to some generic airport, you looked at them in search of some whiff of the past—you looked for a cute one, someone who might like you more than the others, someone to whom you pretended you might give your phone number. You wanted to consider these possibilities but chances are those possibilities simply weren't there. She's not in your league. Her sole education requirement is a GED. She's some bizarre relic. And, like the fact that your flight was oversold and delayed and some used-car salesman in a Wal-Mart suit inexplicably ended up seated next to you in business class, you are more than a little heartbroken about the whole thing. This is because the sex appeal of the flight attendant, like the sex appeal of flying, is gone forever. As much as you act like you have it over her, you somehow still long for an earlier era, back when there was no question that she had it over you.

The sky is a strange place to be. Eustachian tubes are tested up here. The human lung is not designed for the air outside. The food is nuked, the forks are plastic, the dirty words have been edited out of the movie. There's a good chance that the flight attendants, who may be hamming it up during the oxygen mask announcement and giggling in the rear galley like sauced-up Tri Delts, have not met each other until they boarded the plane.

When I board an evening flight on US Airways from Philadelphia to San Francisco, accompanied by a flight attendant who agreed to participate in a magazine article, no one else on the crew has met me or had any warning that I'd be coming along. I tell them that I am writing a story about flight attendants for a glossy men's magazine (the story, in the end, was killed by the editor because it lacked the prurient details he'd hoped for). After a few requests that I change their names—"I want to be called Lola!"—we are getting along like old high school pals. They're connoisseurs of bonding, high skilled socializers. If a reporter showed up to my workplace and announced that she'd be there for the next thirty-six hours I'd duck out for coffee and never come back. But there's plenty of coffee here already. They can't leave and their ability to deal with this fact is pretty much Job One.

This is called a turnaround, a day-and-a-half stint during which this crew will fly from their base in Philadelphia to San Francisco and then to Charlotte before returning to Philadelphia. We are on a Boeing 757— a "seven-five," in airline speak. All of the flight attendants are in their thirties or forties, four are women, three of whom are married, and two are men. All have been flying for at least ten years.

To contemplate what it means to be a flight attendant for ten or more years is to consider, after getting past the initially ludicrous notion of serving drinks at 37,000 feet, the effects of the relatively recent, popular tendency to put flying in a category that also includes walking and driving. To say that flight has become pedestrian is something of a Yogi Berra-ism. But to say that air travel has infused itself into the human experience without leaving marks or building up potentially problematic immunities is to view technology in a Pollyanna-like manner that may have gone out of fashion when applied to phenomena like the Internet and surveillance cameras but continues to thrive in the realm of travel. When it comes to technology's hold on our quality of life, cyber porn may be insidious, but jetliners are by now almost quaint, older than Peter, Paul, and Mary, as common as the telephone.

This is true and not true, a dilemma that often emerges when, as is the case in air travel, the glorious evolves into the stultifying and we are forced to come up with ways to re-experience, if not the original novelty, some form of entertainment. This is where the flight attendant appears onstage. When flying began, she was part of the show, as slick as the aircraft itself. Even through the 1970s, passengers were moneyed and expensively outfitted; ladies wore gloves on DC-4s. To deplane using a movable staircase was, for a moment, to do as rock stars and presidents did, and respect was paid accordingly. The idea has always been that the persona of the flight attendants should reflect that of the flying public.

In that respect, little has changed. The only difference is that today the flying classes seem a little more public than in the past. The flight attendant, too, is given to the bad manicures and bad perms of any girl next door. She's still part of the entertainment, it's just that this is a lower-budget production. This may gnaw at passengers, but those holding $99 tickets to Miami may do well to look at the larger picture. Perhaps the flight attendant wouldn't remind us so glumly of the girl next-door if so many of us didn't live close to the airport.

Still, passengers pay attention to flight attendants, not during the safety announcements, when they're supposed to, but later, while flight attendants are eating dinner or reading *Cosmo* or doing normal things that are somehow rendered out of sync because of the uniform. During our five hours and twenty-six minutes to San Francisco, we hit some "light chop" twice—airlines discourage pilots from using the word "turbulence," which frightens passengers—and the seat belt sign goes on. Passengers get up anyway. They visit the flight attendants in the galleys. They ask for playing cards and more drinks and hand over their garbage to be thrown out. Wayward business travelers amble around the first-class galley and take stabs at the same kinds of conversations they impose on people sitting next to them. "Where do you live? Do you like it there?" and then "Could you get me another drink?"

Even as he accepts an empty pretzel bag from an unshaven, Reebok-wearing passenger, Carl, who is working in the main cabin tonight, manages to put a spin on his role as service provider. "We're a few notches below celebrity status," he says. "The moment people see a crew member, their eyes are on you constantly. People will come into the galley and just stare while you eat dinner. You have to watch everything do you and say."

Carl is thirty-six and has been a flight attendant with US Airways for twelve years. I am asking him questions in the aft galley ("aft" is used to describe anything located behind the wings) where he and Jim, his friend and colleague, have fashioned a seat for me out of a stack of plastic crates because I'm not allowed to sit in the flight attendant-reserved jump seat. They have poured salad dressing left over from first class into a plastic cup and are eating it off of their fingers. "We have a needy bunch tonight," Carl says. "But not as bad as if we were going to L.A. Certainly nothing like Florida."

A lot of call buttons have been ringing tonight. A lot of people cannot seem to figure out how to use their headsets to watch the in-flight screening of *Tomorrow Never Dies*. A fleshy, spacy eleven-year-old boy repeatedly visits the aft galley asking for more soda, more peanuts, some ice cream. "You're a pretty demanding kid," Carl says with just enough smirk so that I notice but the kid does not. Carl and Jim disagree as to whether the boy qualifies for the unofficial passenger shit list that is compiled on every flight.

"He's a pain in the ass," says Carl.

"No, he's obviously slow," says Jim. "I feel sorry for him."

Still, no one is punching anyone in the nose tonight. No one has threatened a flight attendant with bodily harm or become obstreperously drunk or engaged in the sort of activity that would merit a presentation of those restraints stored in the cockpit. The fact that these sorts of incidents are ascending at an alarmingly steep angle, mostly for those pesky reasons having to do with the invasion of a public mentality into what was once perceived as a private space, dominates much of what is written and discussed about flight attendants these days. It is part of the reason that I am here in the aft galley dipping my finger in salad dressing tonight, the other part having to do with discerning whether the deglamorization of the job is the cause or the symptom of all that aggression.

What is at first most noticeable about flight attendants is the chronic disorientation that follows them both on and off the job. With work space measured by aisle widths and hours either stolen or protracted by virtue of time changes and date lines, flight attendants occupy a personal space that must prove stronger than the artificial and ever-changing scope of "real" time and geography. Flight attendants are always tired and usually bored and, though they are required to wear a working watch at all times, understand distinctly the difference between knowing what time it is and feeling what time it is. A forty-five minute break on a transatlantic flight demands the ability to fall asleep instantly on the jump seat. They must learn to literally sleep on cue.

But there is another layer in the psyche of flying that transcends the burdensome working conditions of flight attendants. It's a set of notions that has a lot to do with life on the ground and yet can best be unpacked by examining the ebb and flow of life on an airplane. Just as air pressure will make one martini in the air equal two on the ground, the malaise of modern life extends its claws in cartoon-like proportions on an airplane. It's a sickness aggravated by tiny bathrooms and recirculating air and laptop computers that allow no excuse to take a break from work. "What I hate is when passengers won't put the computer away when I try to bring them dinner," Theresa, a sinewy Mexican-American flight atten-dant for US Airways, tells me. She is in the first-class galley eating choco-late syrup out of a plastic cup. "They never look up, never take a break to enjoy the flight. They never just look out the window and see how beautiful it is."

This is a disease of plastic and its discontents. It is what happens when sleep becomes a greater novelty than gravity defiance. It is what happens when the concept of New York to London seems more like changes in a movie set than a journey involving thousands of miles of empty sky, five degrees of longitude, an ocean. It is what happens when the miraculous becomes the mundane, when we are no longer amazed by flying but bored by it at best and infuriated by it more often than not. And it is this hybrid of nonchalance and aggression that has largely come to define the modern air traveler. It's what causes passengers to punch, slap, spit, swear, make obscene gestures, grope, and fling food at flight attendants and each other. It's what makes people dismantle smoke detectors, throw tantrums when they don't get a meal choice, and threaten to get a crew member fired over such infractions as not having cranberry juice. That the flight attendant must act as an agent for the big, impenetrable aircraft as well as for the small, vulnerable passenger is both a corporate conflict and a metaphysical conundrum. As boring as the airplane may be at this point, its technology remains distancing and unnerving, sometimes even terrifying. And whether the flight attendant is aware of it or not, her duty is to bridge the gap between the artificiality of the cabin and the authentic human impulses that play themselves out in that cabin. She has to shake her ass yet still know how to open the exit door.

The more tangible reasons for her condition have to do with numbers. Every year more seats are squeezed on to planes, seat width has become narrower, flights are oversold, and cheap tickets attract passengers that would otherwise be taking the bus. Flight attendants blame the overcrowding on federal deregulation, which occurred in 1978, and essentially legislated that airlines were allowed to spend as little money as possible per flight as long as they did not violate federal safety standards. This introduced significantly lower ticket prices; it costs an average of twenty-four percent less to fly today than before deregulation.

Out of this was born the era of the $99 ticket. It also meant an abrupt end to luxury air travel; the pillbox hats were traded in for unwashed hair. "We're taught in training that people can't get on board if they have curlers in their hair or no shoes on," said Tracy, another US Airways flight attendant. "And if they have to publish that [in training manuals], that's frightening."

"They show up wearing jogging suits," Carl says. "And I doubt that they're wearing any underwear under those things."

"I hate it when people in the exit row put their feet up on the bulkhead," a Delta flight attendant told me a few weeks later. "If you were a guest in someone's house, would you put your feet on the wall?"

It seems like such a small complaint, but then again this is the sort of gesture that shapes the psyches of those who work in the air. This is *not* her house. And yet it is. This is not a house at all, and yet it's the place where a huge number of people spend a huge amount of time. As more and more Americans carry the detritus of earthbound life to this tube in the air, measures must be taken to make them feel at home without allowing the frontier to become lawless. "When the door closes, we must play every role," said Britt Marie Swartz, a Delta flight attendant who began her career at Pan Am in the late 1970s and actually cooked eggs to order in 747 galleys. "We're doctors, lawyers, travel agents, therapists, waitresses, and cops. No one would demand all of that from a normal person."

The first thing aspiring flight attendants learn when they attend a recruitment meeting at the American Airlines training school near the

Dallas/Fort Worth airport is that, if hired, they will make a base starting salary of around $14,000 a year. The second thing they must do is fill out a lengthy questionnaire designed to give recruiters an idea of their basic character makeup. When I visit the training facility, I am not allowed to see this questionnaire, although I am told that the nature of their answers will lead to what interviewers call "probing points," wherein candidates are asked to talk about themselves in ways that may or may not indicate personality traits incompatible with airplane social dynamics. "There was one grammar outburst," a recruiter says as he emerges from an interview. "I think I detected a double negative." Although I must sign a release saying that I will not print or repeat any of the questions asked of candidates, I am allowed to print the answers they give. And as I spend an hour watching a sweet and painfully sincere twenty-four-year-old from Arkansas hang herself on the basis of about two answers, I am amazed at what an art the recruiters (all of whom are former or working flight attendants) have made out of selecting their co-workers. The candidate, carefully outfitted in an Arkansas version of a power suit, complete with Fayva-type pumps and a neckerchief, seals her fate based on the following responses:

"I would say 'I don't find that type of humor funny' and walk out of the galley," and, "If nothing else worked, I wouldn't lie. I guess I would say, 'Your feet seem to be causing an odor. Can you please put your shoes back on?'"

The woman is sent back to Arkansas with the promise that she will be notified by letter within six weeks, which means that she most certainly will never be hired. Though the recruiter, who looks and speaks almost exactly like the weatherman on my local ABC television affiliate, cannot put his finger directly on what turned him off to her, he tells me it has something to do with apparent inflexibility.

During the week that I observe training, I spend most of my time with a class of sixty students. They have been selected from an original pool of 112,000 applicants, all but 4,000 of whom were eliminated via an automated telephone screening system. American has one of the most rigorous training programs in the industry—flight attendants from other carriers frequently refer to them as the "Sky Nazis"—but it is also among the most sought-after employers, both for its reputation and its pay scale, which is high by industry standards.

The training facility is an awe-inspiring complex. Occupying a large building next door to the flight academy, it contains a hotel, conference center, and salon, as well as a multitude of offices, lecture halls, and several life-size cabin simulators. The simulators, which fill up large rooms, look like movie sets of airplanes. They hold real seats, real galleys, and real doors. The windows are filled in with painted renderings of fluffy white clouds. The flight attendants practice serving real food to their classmates and are observed closely by their instructors. Part of their training involves getting accustomed to erratic hours and last-minute schedule changes; their day can begin as early as 3 A.M., and individual students often receive telephone calls in the classroom from a mock scheduling unit, which informs them that drills or simulated flight times have been reassigned. Business attire must be worn at all times. This means jackets and ties for the men and no skirts above the knee for tje women. Flight attendants both in and outside of American have referred to this training program as Barbie Boot Camp. New hires consult at least once with the American Airlines salon manager, who suggests suitable hairstyles—the French twist is especially popular—and teaches the women how to apply makeup, which is to be worn at all times during training. Several of the students privately refer to the image consultant as Sergeant Lipstick, who is known to keep tabs on the freshness of application.

Throughout the week I am escorted at all times by a representative from the corporate communications office, an impeccably groomed and perfectly nice woman who leads me through an itinerary that has been set up specifically for me. Almost all of the classes I observe have to do with aircraft evacuation. One class involves food service, another is centered almost entirely around a device called the Automated External Defibrillator, which American recently acquired for most of their overseas jets and which, I am told several times, many other airlines do not have. To my disappointment, I have apparently missed the phase of training that involves personal appearance standards. When I ask twice if I can relocate to the hotel at the training center in order to interview the experienced flight attendants who are housed here for their annual recurrent training, I am subtly put off both times; like a demanding passenger, I am denied my request without ever hearing the word "no."

It seems to me that flight attendant training has relatively little to do with the actual job of flight attendant. Although the trainees have ostensibly been hired based on a vibrancy of personality and the good sense not to say "I don't find that type of humor funny," there is something so sterile about the vibe of this education that it's hard to imagine how their lessons will ever mesh with the reality of dealing with actual people in the actual sky. In an entire week of observing classes, I never once hear the word "crash." Instead, a strange semantic code seems to be in place. Several times I hear the term "crispy critter," which, apparently, is what the flight attendants will be if they can't maneuver a clear path through fire. "If you do not go through the protected area and there's a fire," chirps an instructor at seven-fifteen one morning, "who's the crispy critter? You!"

Though American may have earned its "Sky Nazi" wings by maintaining a somewhat overzealous tone when it comes to corporate culture, their personnel bear little resemblance to the "coffee, tea, or me" drones of the past. Recruiters say that they work hard to hire crews that will reflect the demographic makeup of the passengers and from the looks of things, they're succeeding. The class I observed had several men and women over forty and a number of people of color, including a thirty-six-year-old former North Carolina highway patrolman with two children who said he just always wanted to fly. "The times that I've felt down about being here, I just go to the airport and watch the planes take off and land," he says in a group interview that's been set up for me by company supervisors.

That's a poetic sentiment, and American Airlines doesn't mind that kind of sound bite. But the theme music they really want played is all about "customer service," a term that the company repeats like a mantra, much like the Boy Scouts' "Be Prepared." Things get tricky, however, when it becomes clear just how difficult it is to uphold Ritz-Carlton-like service philosophies in an arena that is accessible to almost all walks of life. Customer service may be the gospel here, but it isn't necessarily the law. "Our company no longer holds fast to the policy that the customer is always right," says Sara Ponte, a flight attendant recruiting supervisor. "If a passenger consistently causes a disturbance, then that's not a passenger we want on our airline." Although no one at American will confirm or deny any rumors, company myths have it that a few celebrities, including Kim Basinger and Charlie Sheen, have been banned from the airline because of in-flight misconduct. Basinger's tantrum was allegedly sparked after she was refused ice cubes made from Evian water.

Herein lies the central conflict of flight attendant training, and it is the conflict that factors most heavily into the larger identity crisis of airborne life. Cabin crews are supposed to maintain an aura of exclusivity by making passengers feel special. But how can this be done when the very customers they're trying to please are anything but exclusive? By definition, the public is not private, nor are flight attendants high-priced personal assistants who consider the maintenance of freshly starched shirts a higher priority than feeding 173 people in under one hour or, for that matter, being able to evacuate 173 people in less than ninety seconds. That airlines continue to advertise themselves as luxury watering holes that, it so happens, will get you across the country in five hours is both a disservice to the flight attendant and one more way that the passenger is distanced from the actual concept of flying. Singapore Airlines, which is considered to have the highest level of customer service of any carrier in the world, has long touted their flight attendants as their major selling point. In the 1980s, the airline's slogan was "Singapore Girl, You're A Great Way to Fly." While it's doubtful than any United States carrier could get away with this kind of ad copy, all flight attendants carry the burden of this kind of public image. They are expected to represent the sex in their airline while remaining utterly nonthreatening. They are symbols of technology and symbols of flesh, and this is where their religion and their rules begin to come unglued.

When new hires are asked to leave American Airline's training program, they always disappear instantly. Students can be eating lunch together only to find a classmate gone permanently an hour later. In this class of sixty, seven left early, some for reasons no one quite understands.

When I try to talk to the students, they happily accommodate my questions until they realize that everything they say will be within earshot of my escort from corporate communications. A woman waiting to practice a drill tells me that she was forced by the company salon to cut her hair and now feels bad about it. Back in the classroom, half an hour later, she clams up on me. When I press her, she finally slips me a note that reads "I can't really talk now."

Though I cannot be sure, I have inklings that my escort from corporate communications is keeping an eye on me when I visit the ladies' room. We eat lunch together every day. We walk down every corridor together. As I throw questions at anyone I can find she lingers next to me, reducing every flight attendant to the bland politeness of the first-class cabin. Though my escort has offered to pick me up at my hotel and drive me to the training center every morning, I have a rental car and assure her that I can find my way on my own. One afternoon, after parting ways in the parking lot, we get separated by a few cars as we pull onto the road that leads to the freeway. As I drive along I notice that she's pulled over to the shoulder so I can catch up. "How nice," I think to myself. "She's making sure I don't get lost." Hours later it occurs to me that she might have been making sure I didn't sneak back to the training center to interview people without her. I had indeed considered staying behind by myself, only to discard the idea for fear I'd be sent home.

Back on our US Airways flight to San Francisco, I learn that Carl and Jim have a penchant, during mid-flight seat belt checks, for taking note of male passengers who have fallen asleep and developed erections. They then go into the galley and whisper something in the neighborhood of "Check out 26C" and send other flight attendants, one by one, to do the old corner-of-the-eye glance while moseying on by. This is considered a necessary distraction and an entirely acceptable way to wile away the hours. They also play a game called "Thirty-Second Review," wherein they have thirty seconds to walk through the cabin and make a note of the seat number of the passenger they would most like to have sex with.

As I research this story, I am told about flight attendants who work as prostitutes on the side, flight attendants who give mid-flight blow jobs to pilots, flight attendants who are transsexuals, and flight attendants who carry separate business cards for their drag queen personae. A friend of mine can tell a story about a flight attendant who gave him a hand job in the business-class section of a 747 during her half-hour break on a flight from New York to São Paulo. A cab driver who took me home from the airport a few months ago described meeting a flight attendant on the way to Orlando and shacking up with her for a week at a hotel near Disney World. "Of course, I had to pay for everything," he said to me as we careened over the Triborough Bridge. "She had it all figured out."

None of these actions or examples, weighed on their own, register enough scandal to send the airlines into collapse. As sensational as some of them are, these are the exceptions that prove the rule that most flight attendants are regular people with regular aspirations, many of which do not require business cards at all. But the fact that such tales are recounted so readily, both by people outside of the job and by flight attendants themselves, reveals a trait that is shared by just about everyone who works in the air. As the remoteness of the sky threatens to render them something less than human, they have no choice but to make themselves almost exaggeratedly human, hyperreal characters who rely on wild behavior and raunchy mythologies in order to outsmart the numbing effects of the airplane.

These stories, apocryphal or not, serve to sustain humanity inside the artificiality of the tube. A particularly dark plotline involves the widely held belief that the so-called Patient Zero, to whom over forty of the first AIDS cases were traced back, was an Air Canada flight attendant named Gaeten Dugas. More common are ambitious passengers seeking membership into the Mile High Club. Carl recalls a couple from Dayton who sheepishly offered him $20 to allow them to enter the lavatory together (he waived the fee). An American Airlines flight attendant recounts what he swears is a "true rumor" about identical twins who worked as flight attendants for Eastern Airlines in the 1980s. The sisters worked together on wide-body aircrafts like the DC-10 and L10-11 that had lower level galleys accessible from small elevators, which could, in effect, be locked by keeping the door open downstairs. Together they would solicit a male passenger and take him down into the galley for clandestine three-way sex. Afterwards, they would serve him champagne.

Such rituals have been in place since the inception of commercial air travel. Pan Am stewardesses regularly taped centerfolds to the backs of safety cards when flying United States troops on military-contracted flights to Vietnam. Even into the late 1970s, flight attendants on Pacific South Airlines wore uniforms that featured miniskirts and go-go boots. The difference today is that these rituals are played out on the sly. As airlines fight harassment and discrimination lawsuits, keeping strict watch over potentially solicitous pilots or questionable behavior on layovers, these antics are mind games more than parlor games. There is considerably more talk than action going on. The influence of gay male culture cannot be ignored either. It is perhaps no accident that stereotypically gay male styles of social behavior seem custom-made for the flight attendant lifestyle. "For a lot of the gay guys it's been a wonderful ride," says Carl, who came out the same year he began flying. "The airlines have been a friendly atmosphere for being ourselves. But it's more social than sexual."

Jim, who is also gay, is quick to jokingly add that there is no better job for him *because* he is gay. This is a valid point, but not in the way that probably first comes to mind. While there are plenty of male flight attendants who are not gay, the cabin is dominated by an unquestionably campy sensibility; the boys help the girls with new hair styles, the girls loudly evaluate the boys' asses. It's a vibe that points toward the tolerance on which flight attendants pride themselves. But it also scratches the itch of their central contradiction. They are at once erotic figures and cartoon characters, raunchy talkers who wouldn't be out of place in the cast of Up With People. Their penis jokes have the ring of a junior high school cafeteria; words like "meat" or "fruit" cannot be spoken without some degree of sophomoric innuendo. Flight attendants live in a state of permanent chaos, and thrive on it. Unlike their passengers, whose systems are still adjusting to the transient new world, the flight attendant has successfully adapted to surroundings that are neither here nor there. For better or worse, she represents the nervous system of the future.

Kew Gardens, Queens, near JFK and LaGuardia airports in New York City, is the sometime-home to approximately two thousand flight attendants and pilots. I visit an apartment complex that houses two hundred of them in dorm-like apartments that are cleanly furnished with drab sofas, Formica dinette sets, and the perfunctory $24 halogen torch lamp. The building's landlord actively seeks out airline personnel, who each pay a monthly rent of $150 for their maximum stays of seven days. Each unit has two or three bedrooms that hold two sets of bunk beds with the exception of the errant, single-occupancy pilot's room, one of which is elaborately outfitted with stereo equipment, a computer, and a wall-mounted, large-screen television affixed with a Post-it that reads "Seinfeld 11:00." A lot of pilots, however, drift in and out of a nearby place nicknamed Animal House, which is considered a prime spot for crew parties and fraternity-style debauchery.

But things are pretty calm tonight in unit C-2, where several flight attendants, many of whom have just returned from places where today is still yesterday, are gathered in the common room watching The Weather Channel. Janet is thirty-eight, divorced, and worked on the ground for Delta until she got a company transfer and began flying in 1993. She commutes to this crash pad from her home in Atlanta, and, like many of her colleagues, admits that her transient lifestyle can get in the way of her personal life. A typically prepubescent maxim in aviation goes like this: "What does AIDS stand for? Airline Induced Divorce Syndrome." For every crew member who relishes the personal space inherent in her job, there is another who feels her relationships have been sabotaged by it.

"A lot of the girls from my class are divorced now," she says, finding herself unable to keep from getting up to refill my drink before I even finish it. "Guys you meet think it's kind of fascinating, the whole mystique of being a flight attendant. I dated a guy who I swear wanted me to wear my uniform when we went out. But they don't really want to have a relationship with someone who is gone so much. They'll come home at five o'clock and you're not there."

Later we go across the street to Airline Night at the local dive bar.

There are hundreds of flight attendants and a few scattered pilots order-
ing two-for-one drinks and rubbing each other's shoulders. Even out of
uniform, there is something about the crowd that is unmistakably air-
liney. With their clean fingernails and neat hair, they seem like they come
from nowhere, as if they're extras in a made-for-TV movie. Like people
in an airport, they are a smorgasbord of regional accents and styles.
Though most will fly together only rarely, they tend to touch each other
a lot, giving bear hugs and wet kisses and pulling familiar figures aside
saying, "I remember you from the seven-two, a couple years ago."

Not unlike the main cabin of an airplane, this bar is jammed with
representatives from every town in every state. Hired to assist and identify with the country's disenfranchised, disoriented air travelers, the primary job requirement seems less about handling an emergency than dif-
fusing the side effects of hours spent in the hothouse that is the plane.
Very few say they fear an accident, and most maintain a Zen-like philosophy about the possibility of crashing. "I figure when it's my time to go,
it's my time to go," a 32-year-old flight attendant named Len says. Of all
the flight attendants I spoke with, about half had experienced incidents
like engine explosions or faulty indicator lights that required returning to the airport. Within that group, only a tiny fraction had ever evac-
uated their plane. Britt Marie Swartz says that early in her Pan Am career
she was scheduled for a trip that she had to cancel at the last minute.
"The plane crashed. After that I was never afraid. I figure my time will
come when it comes."

No one is allowed to die on an airplane. The worst thing you can do
to a flight attendant is try to die on her. It won't work. She'll have to give
you CPR no matter how evident your passing may be. Upon making

an emergency landing, after they cart you away, the plane will be impounded. There will be the inevitable lawsuits.

"We are told unofficially that no one is allowed to die on the airplane," a Delta flight attendant in Kew Gardens told me. "Maybe they died on the jetway, but not on the airplane." Flight attendants are not allowed to declare death, and doctors, if there are any on board, are often reluctant to speak up when called for because of liability issues. In 1997, Lufthansa lost a one-million-dollar lawsuit against the family of a man who had died of a heart attack on the plane.

There is an unparalleled creepiness about airplane deaths, perhaps because we most often associate them with the gothic horror of news footage when there is a crash. But while air crashes occupy a far larger place in the popular imagination than they do in realistic odds, medical emergencies are relatively common. Every flight attendant in this story described situations which were sometimes harrowing enough to rival an episode of *ER*—strokes, seizures, childbirth, psychotic reactions to drugs, broken bones, a catheter that needed to be changed in heavy turbulence.

In the sky, denial is not just human instinct, it's a job requirement. A flight attendant for Canadian Airlines remembers an elderly man who, unbeknownst to his wife, died in his sleep. "I put a blanket on him," she says. "His wife was right beside him and I let her believe he was asleep until we landed. It was the best thing to do given the situation."

"A colleague of mine said that last week a woman traveling with her husband knew he had died twenty minutes into the flight," says Shannon Veedock, a Chicago-based American Airlines flight attendant. "They had made a stop in Dallas, stayed on the plane, and continued on to New York. She kept telling the crew he was asleep. She'd even called her son from the plane and told him what was going on. She was determined to get him home."

Here again lies the contradiction of flying, smatterings of the grotesque on a sublime canvas, heroism one minute and *Beavis and Butt-Head* behavior the next. A flight attendant with a major airline explains to me how she and her co-workers spent two hours and forty-five minutes giving CPR to a passenger who was vomiting on them and saved his life. Five minutes later in our conversation she recalls a particularly nasty passenger who demanded an extra lime for her gin and tonic. "She'd been snapping her fingers at other crew members, snapping her fingers at me, and so I took her glass into the galley, got two pieces of lime and shoved them up my nostrils and wiggled them around. Then I plopped them back in the glass and cheerfully brought it back to her."

The night I am flying home from my turnaround with the US Airways crew, I find myself overtaken with an uncontrollable urge to become a flight attendant, to join the living up here among the sleeping, to wear the uniform. It's the uniform that gets me where I live, that hideous, dazzling, itchy ensemble of unnatural fibers, that homage to country and corporation. It embodies all the contradictions of airplane life, contradictions which, in the end, make more evident the crisis of national identity: the need to be free versus the need to be sewn inside an organized structure. With their insignia and their rebellion, I can't help but think that flight attendants are, in a sense, quintessential Americans. They are at once rootless souls and permanent fixtures, vagabonds who can't stay anywhere too long and plain folks trying to restore equilibrium to a crowded, light-headed world.

This 757 is a tube of intersecting lives, a pressurized cross section of the entire population, a flying nation. In a few hours we will land at an airport that looks like a shopping mall. We will stay in a hotel that gives no clue as to what city we're in. In a world whose pace and legroom is controlled by the speed of technology, a glance down this length of darkened cabin gives a pretty fair indication of the shape we're in. One hundred ninety-four passengers are curled up asleep in what little space they have, their coats tucked under their heads, their knees tucked under their chins. Laptop computer screens are glowing. The air smells of coffee and peanuts and bodies. It's such a specific aroma, bottled in its giant container, sponged off the skins of 194 people who think it must be coming from the person sitting next to them. But this is what an airplane always smells like. It is the scent of the house where the entire world lives.

TOY CHILDREN

Though I had a stuffed-animal collection that rivaled the inventory of a Toys "R" Us, I was a child who hated dolls. By "hate," I'm not talking about a cool indifference. I'm talking about a palpable loathing, a dislike so intense that my salient memory of doll ownership concerns a plastic baby whose duty among my playthings consisted solely of being thrown against the wall repeatedly and then smudged with a combination of red lipstick, purple Crayola, and, when available, spaghetti sauce. This was done in an effort to simulate severe injury, possibly even internal bleeding, and this doll, who, if I recall correctly, had eyes that opened and shut and therefore had come preassigned with the name Baby Drowsy, spent most of her time in a shoe box in my closet. This was the intensive care unit, the place where, when I could no longer stand the sight of Baby Drowsy's fat, contusion-ridden face, I would Scotch-tape a folded Kleenex to her forehead and announce to my mother that Baby Drowsy had been in yet another massive car wreck. I would then proceed to tend with painstaking care to my thirty-plus animals, all of whom I had personally christened with names like Excellent Eagle, Mr. Nice, and Soft Koala, and who, I was entirely certain, could communicate with both myself and each other through a complex telepathy. I say complex because, even at five, I had the ability to convey my thoughts to individual animals and then conference-in others should the discussion be relevant. They could do the same when they talked amongst themselves. Eyeore could discuss the events of the day with Squiffy. Peter Panda could alert Bunny Rabbit that he had fallen behind the bed. Everyone knew about Baby Drowsy's frequent mishaps. And none of us really cared. In the social hierarchy of my bedroom, animals ranked highest. Dolls were somewhere between dust balls and cockroaches. They were uninvited guests that gathered in the corners, something to be stomped on.

But since I was a girl, I had dolls. People gave them to me, though Baby Drowsy was unquestionably subject to the most abuse. Something about the word "drowsy" struck me as flaccid, even masochistic; it was as if drowsy was baby talk for "drown me," and the beatings seemed to emerge out of a sense that she was asking for it. The handful of other dolls had the luck of being simply ignored. I had a Raggedy Ann, whose stuffed-animal-like properties redeemed her enough so that she would occasionally be placed next to—though never in the pile with—the dogs and bears. My mother, perhaps worried about whatever maternal instincts were failing to develop in me, spent several years trying to find a doll I might actually like. With chubby baby dolls clearly out of the question, she tried to introduce me to more sophisticated dolls, older girls in higher quality plastic, dolls with hair to be brushed and tasteful clothes to be changed. Nothing amused me. I loved my animals, furry, long-tongued creatures who were safe from the hair-braiding, cradle-rocking proclivities of playmates, some of whom had the hubris, not to mention the bad sense, to bring their own dolls with them when visiting my house. By the time I was old enough to enter into the world of Barbies, my mother's quest to make a nurturer of me was subsumed by her feminist impulses. I was given no Barbies and received stuffed animals every Christmas until I was approximately twenty-seven.

While it might seem that my intense dislike for dolls is simply a dramatic manifestation of my intense affection for animals, I suspect that the whole doll issue is part of a larger semiotic equation, an entire genre of girlhood—and childhood in general—that I could just never get with. While I can't say that I had an unhappy childhood, I was unhappy being a child. Just as there has not been a morning of my adult life when I don't wake up and thank the gods that I am no longer a kid, there was hardly a day between the ages of three and eighteen that I didn't yearn for the time when I would be grown-up. Aside from the usual headaches of being a kid—the restricted freedoms, the semi-citizenship—what really ailed me were the trappings of kid-dom: the mandatory hopscotch, the inane cartoons, the cutesy names ascribed to daycare centers and recreation programs, like Little Rascals Preschool and Tiny Tot Tumbling. Why was a simple burger and fries called The Lone Ranger? Why did something as basic as food have to be repackaged to resemble a toy? Even as a child I resented this lowbrow aesthetic—the alphabet-block designs on everything, the music-box soundtrack, the relentless kitsch of it all.

Dolls are the ultimate symbol of childhood; they are toy children. Though I realize that playing with dolls is supposed to mimic the adult act of caring for children, playing with dolls always struck me as nothing more but childhood squared, a child doing a childish thing with a simulacrum of a child. It was like some hideous vortex. Adults think it's cute when girls burp their dolls. We buy them dolls that cry, and dolls that pee. I think there's even a doll that spits up. Most people see this as endearing, even healthy in a biological imperative sense. I see it as an exercise in narcissism. But I suppose that says more about me than about the doll-buying public or the doll-diapering girls who are supposedly doing the thing that comes naturally to them but just didn't to me.

I read somewhere that women who choose not to have children are more likely to have grown up preferring stuffed animals to dolls. Though I'm probably still too young to make pronouncements about my wish to forgo motherhood, I must say that, at thirty, my desire for children is all but nil. Though it's not impossible for me to enjoy other people's kids, my biological clock seems to reside permanently in a time zone to my west. Babies amuse me only mildly, toddlers not at all, and children of the talking, television-watching, Happy-Meal-eating variety fill me with a kind of queasy empathy. When I see a mother with her child, I identify not with the adult but with the small person who, in my mind, seems trapped in a world governed by romanticized, consumer-driven notions of childhood. I see a kid and I think to myself, "I'm sorry you have to be a kid right now. I'm sorry you have to play with Legos. I'm sorry you have to ride in the back seat."

A psychiatrist would see this as regressive. A lot of other people would argue that childhood is about as pure as anything gets, that the preadolescent mind enjoys some kind of blissful exemption from adult concerns, and that little girls and, when given the opportunity, little boys, gravitate naturally towards dolls. Dolls, say the experts, are merely objects on which to practice the care-giving skills we need to survive as a species.

Though I can understand that, I still can't relate to it. To me, a child with a doll is a child who has been railroaded by the trappings of childhood. She has already acquired her first accessory, an inanimate version of herself, one that possibly even requires batteries. She has already tied up one hand, already spent more time looking down than looking around. You might ask how I make a distinction between the dreaded doll and the adored stuffed animal. Why is it that I can smile at the child with a bear but always end up pitying the child with a doll? Perhaps it's because animals are more closely connected with the imaginative world than dolls are. They are ageless, genderless, and come in colors that defy nature. To play with a stuffed panda, or, in my case, to telepathically communicate with one, is a creative act. To play with a doll is to stare yourself in the face, to gaze at an object that is forever trapped in infancy. Maybe that's why dolls frighten me so much. Forever trapped in babyhood, they threaten the very essence of life's possibilities. They're my greatest nightmare come true. They never, ever grow up.

According To The Women

I'm Fairly Pretty

I have always had a problem with science fiction and fantasy enthusiasts. Of all the subcultures that, for various neurotic reasons, provoke my disdain, none seem to bridle me quite as much as those comprised of people who appear to have forfeited real life for something they're likely to characterize as "a quest." Granted, my scope is limited. My associations with people involved in fantasy games and other pagan-oriented pursuits are confined to certain members of the high school science-fiction club who wore "Question Reality" buttons and the Society for Creative Anachronism types at my college who reenacted medieval battles on the grass outside the dormitories. These groups provide what is perhaps the only example of social harassment that actually gets worse as you get older. In the high school lunch room we merely laughed behind the sci-fi kids' backs. In college, I once stood idly by as someone poured beer out a fourth-floor dormitory window onto the velvet cape of a jouster who called himself "Leaf Blackthorn" and felt no guilt.

This wasn't supposed to be a story about geek love. This was supposed to be a story about a group of people in northern California who practice a way of life known as "polyamory." As any seventh grade Latin student could probably infer, polyamory means "many loves." Polyamorous people, or "polys," as they call themselves, love many, many people. And a poly doesn't just love those people, he or she has sex with them, even when some of those people live in the same house and are married to still other people in that house, many of whom the afore-mentioned poly is already having sex with anyway.

The most public polyamorous family in the United States is called Ravenheart. They took the name Ravenheart three years ago when they were living on a remote California ranch surrounded by ravens. They also invented the word "polyamory," combining the Greek and Latin roots for "many loves," and it has since been entered into the Oxford English Dictionary. None of the Ravenhearts are related by birth. In polyamorous terminology, they are known as "a nest," a chosen family. Today they occupy a large house and an adjacent smaller house (which has four apartment units and often houses friends and other lovers) in Sonoma County, about forty-five miles north of San Francisco. There are three men, all heterosexual, and three women, all bisexual. They have an age range spanning over thirty years. As members of the Church of All Worlds, a neo-pagan religion based on Robert A. Heinlein's 1961 sci-ence fiction novel *Stranger in a Strange Land*, which the eldest family member, Oberon Zell Ravenheart, founded back in 1962, they are allowed to marry more than one partner via a pagan ritual called a hand fasting. And although their coupling arrangements are best out-lined with a map or flowchart, a description of whom sleeps with who goes something like this.

Oberon, fifty-seven, has been legally married to his wife Morning Glory, fifty-three, for twenty-six years. In 1996, they celebrated a hand fasting with a man named Wolf, thirty-six, who just this past August for-mally married a woman named Wynter, twenty-one. Though Oberon and Wolf refer to themselves as each other's husbands—"I can't imagine life without my husband Wolf," Oberon says—and Morning Glory and Wynter consider themselves each other's wives, only Morning Glory and Wynter have sex with each other, although Morning Glory also has sex with Oberon and Wolf. When Wynter became an official Ravenheart three years ago, she had a brief sexual relationship with Oberon, which has since moved into what Oberon describes as a "mentor/apprentice" dynamic. Oberon also has sex at least twice a week with Liza, forty-six, who is also the lover of Jon, twenty-one. The Ravenhearts get regular tests for STDs and the most enforced house rule is that any sex occurring outside the family must involve the use of condoms.

Before I met the Ravenhearts, my knowledge of them was limited mostly to the above information. Oberon sent me biographical sketches of each family member, which explained more or less who is partnered with whom. I knew that they belonged to the Church of All Worlds, but, as my assignment involved gaining an understanding of polyamory and exploring the feasibility or non-feasibility of open multiple partnerships for the vast majority of us, I more or less ignored the pagan stuff.

But when I meet Oberon, who opens the gate to the privacy fence and greets me with a hug, I see his black T-shirt reading "Never Thirst" (one of the big tropes from *Stranger in a Strange Land*) and realize that I have stepped into that realm that has long elicited my deepest repulsion. I have stepped into an intersection of science fiction geeks and velvet-caped jousters. And there is absolutely no separating the family's prolific sexual activity with the fact that they attend ritual events with names like Eleusinian Mysteries and have culled the bulk of their personal philosophies from science fiction novels.

"I never had the slightest glimmerings of monogamy as a personal value," says Oberon, who grew up in the 1940s and 50s in what he calls an "Ozzie and Harriet" family in the suburbs of Chicago. Oberon talks like Timothy Leary and looks like Papa Smurf. He has long gray hair, a long gray beard, and tends to pepper his philosophical musings with references to popular movies and Crosby, Stills & Nash songs. He says that a lyric from David Crosby's "Triad"—"sisters, lovers, water brothers, and in time, maybe others"—pretty much sums up his and Morning Glory's marriage vows. And of course there's an implicit poly message in "Love the One You're With."

"Did you see the movie *Pleasantville*?" Oberon asks. "I thought it was really excellent. My childhood was very much in that era. But my models were characters in stories, in myths. In science fiction there were all these models, all these alternatives, and all you had to do was choose to live that way. I imprinted my ideas of romance and sexuality not from popular romance and literature, but from science fiction and fantasy, where you could do anything you wanted to."

"I probably have more sex than your average porn star," says Wolf Ravenheart. "But it's not that our drive is higher. Our availability of sexual partners is probably pretty high. Right now there are probably a dozen people who I could go out and have a fling with. My biggest problem that I have is how to say no gracefully. Because according to the women I'm fairly pretty. I get a lot of offers."

We are sitting around the coffee table in the family's living room. It has high ceilings, exposed beams, and lots of goddess posters and ceramic figurines, many of which are creations of Mythic Images, the family statuary business. At thirty-six, Wolf looks a lot like what you'd expect someone named Wolf to look like; long wavy brown hair, beard, thick eyebrows growing together in the center. He's what's known as a "gamer," meaning he likes to get together with friends and play games like *Civilization* and *Space 1889*, which fall under the larger umbrella of *Dungeons & Dragons*-style role-playing games. He wears square-shaped metal-framed glasses onto which he clips plastic flip-up shades. When I first meet him he is wearing a T-shirt imprinted with a mythical image accompanied by the words "Winter Is Coming." I can't get up the nerve to ask if the words are a winking double entendre referring to his new bride, Wynter. The Ravenhearts have a calendar hanging on their kitchen wall on which they write their "sleep schedule." It is crammed with names and dates and times, crossed out and rewritten again and again.

"The sleep schedule came out of a desperate need to know where our beds were going to be that night," says Morning Glory. "We needed some kind of stability. So we had some family meetings where we sat down and kind of broke down the week. We tried to figure out a place where everybody had somebody that they wanted to sleep with at least once or twice a week and that they also got time alone."

"Typically during the week I will sleep with Morning Glory on Mondays and Tuesdays," says Wolf. "Wednesdays every other week I'm out of town. I have friends in Sacramento. I game with them and come back Thursday morning. Typically Wynter and I are together Thursday and Friday. Weekends are always chaotic, often there's a festival or something. I have occasional dates with my girlfriend in San Francisco, about once a month. I try to get at least about one night to myself a week. Otherwise, I go nuts."

"Monday and Tuesday nights Liza and Oberon are together," Morning Glory explains. "But Liza and Jon are going away to the Loving More conference this weekend and then they're going to the Zeg community summer camp so it's important that Liza and Oberon get some time to spend together. And Wolf has been ill with the flu so he and I have been kind of not together. So normally I would have been alone. But last night Wynter had a date canceled with her outside boyfriend so she came to me and said, 'Hey, how about we have a date?'"

Sometimes Morning Glory, Wolf, and Wynter get together and have sex. Sometimes Morning Glory, Wolf, and Oberon have sex. Part of the reason family members tend not to inquire about what sex is like between other people is that they know what it's like. They've been there.

"Wynter doesn't ask me what I do with Morning Glory because she's been there many, many times," says Wolf. "There's nothing I know about sex with Morning Glory that she doesn't."

And although a great deal of their conversation revolves around the topic of sex—"For us, sex is like going to the grocery store," says Wolf—the Ravenhearts don't come down for breakfast and spill every detail of the previous night's encounter. "We talk amongst ourselves about our desires and about what turns us on," says Wolf. "But we don't just get up in the morning and chew the fat about what went on. Someone might say 'Hey, it sounds like you broke a chandelier last night,' but that's about it."

It should be noted that the Ravenhearts are not swingers. "The primary difference between the swingers community and the poly community is not so much their sexual practice but that their swinging is a purely discreet sexual activity," says Morning Glory. "With polyamory, it permeates every aspect of our lives."

That means that the Ravenhearts have what amounts to scores of in-laws. Their families, for the most part, accept their living arrangement. Morning Glory and Oberon both have grown children, though not by each other. Wolf has an eight-year-old daughter who lives with her (non-poly) mother in Texas. Family relations seem amazingly unstrained. When I visited the Ravenhearts in August of 2000, Wolf's daughter had just returned to her home in Texas after staying with the family for six weeks. He had given up his room for her, which didn't cause too much inconvenience since he only sleeps in it one night a week.

All of the Ravenhearts have their own bedrooms, except for Oberon, who uses the Mythic Images office as his personal space and floats from room to room as the schedule dictates. The family members stress again and again that the schedule is "fluid," that if someone is not in the mood for a date with a particular person there's no obligation to keep it. They're also allowed to stop sleeping with someone if they want to, although the implication is that they'll eventually start up again.

"I think someone would just say, 'I'm entering a nonsexual phase in our relationship for a while and we just need to be in that space for a while,'" says Morning Glory. "And everyone needs to be okay with that if they're given that message. And what's nice is that there's always someone else in the family who can take up the slack so you're not just totally left out in the cold."

Not that it happens very often.

"We're all here because we've chosen to be here," says Morning Glory. "We've made a commitment to each other."

"People talk about commitment and assume that we must not be interested in it, but the thing is we love commitment," says Oberon. "The hard thing is finding other people who want to make commitments to us."

Though the present incarnation of the Ravenhearts was just a glimmer in Morning Glory's and Oberon's eyes when they met back in 1973, they made it clear from the start that they wanted such a family. The scene was the third-annual Gnostic Aquarian Festival, a psychic phenomena conference in Minneapolis. Oberon was delivering a lecture on the Gaia thesis. Morning Glory had hitchhiked to the conference from Eugene, Oregon, where she was living on a commune with her husband and four-year-old daughter. Though she had an open marriage—"that was the only way I would have ever agreed to be with anyone," she says— her husband was less enthusiastically poly than she was. "I had a lot of other lovers and he had occasional ones that I would engineer for him so he wouldn't be left out," she says. "But he wasn't really interested in being with anybody but me."

After Oberon's lecture, he and Morning Glory felt that they were pulled toward each other by a magnetic force. She leapt from her chair and ran up to him. He immediately took her hand and they walked out of the room where they had what Morning Glory calls "a telepathic communion." They stared at each other for five or ten minutes without speaking, yet they managed to silently convey to each other the sum total of their entire lives.

"We kissed and touched and just connected, and it was clear that we were going to be together," Morning Glory says. She knew that she was in love with Oberon and that she wanted to be in his life. But she had a husband and a child. Moreover, she says, she had a commitment to nonmonogamy and she felt she had to tell him that right away.

"I said to him 'I know what we have is really unique and special and I really want to be with you for the rest of my life,'" says Morning Glory. "'But there's something really important about myself that I have to tell you. If what you want is a monogamous relationship I can't give that to you. It's not in my nature. I never planned to just meet someone and get divorced and dump all the rest of my lovers.' And the look on his face! It was like 'I finally found her!'"

Within twenty-four hours, Morning Glory and Oberon decided to get married at the next Gnostic Aquarian convention in six months. "We were so gaga," Morning Glory says. "We couldn't be separated long enough to go pee."

For the next twenty-two years, Morning Glory and Oberon shared lovers and friends. From 1983 to 1994, they were in an open triad relationship with another woman who had a child, which they all raised together. In 1993, Morning Glory met Wolf at a Pagan Halloween gathering in Tennessee. He was living in Houston at the time and working at Kinko's. For two years they had a long-distance relationship. "Wolf and I would have phone sex," Morning Glory says.

"And after she'd hang up she and I would have wild sex!" Oberon says, interrupting her.

When Morning Glory visited Wolf in Houston for the first time, she walked into his house and knew he would form the perfect triad with her and Oberon. "I looked around and I started laughing internally," she says. "There were the same books on the shelves [that Oberon had], the same comic books, astronomy books, old Star Trek episodes. He had the only other Klingon knife that I'd seen in my life other than Oberon's. And Wolf came out and stayed and we found a really great unit."

In 1995, Wolf moved to California to join Oberon and Morning Glory and the three of them were married in a triad hand-fasting ceremony. This was around the time that Oberon met Liza through a mutual lover. Liza was living on the East Coast at the time, but she fell in love with Oberon and a year later she moved to California. At that point, they were a group of four, but as blissful as life was, something was still missing. Though Morning Glory and Wolf were deeply in love, they knew they weren't soul mates (Oberon is Morning Glory's soul mate), and Morning Glory was always on the lookout for a soul mate for Wolf. She also happened to be in the market for another female partner for herself. Then a young woman named Wynter, who had been raised in the area by poly parents, showed up on Morning Glory's doorstep seeking work at Mythic Images.

"She was the woman I'd been looking for my whole life," says Morning Glory. "We realized we were each other's missing female component."

Morning Glory and Wynter developed a friendship that gradually turned into romantic love. "She was just seventeen at the time so we had to do a lot of sitting on our hands and working out things with her mom and dad and stuff like that," says Morning Glory. "And she ended up coming to work for me as an employee, and it wasn't until she was fully legal that we were able to act on anything."

In the meantime, however, something even more amazing happened. Morning Glory introduced Wynter to Wolf at the pagan May Day celebration, a sexual erotic energy festival. They fell in love instantly and turned out to be soul mates. Wynter formally entered the family in 1997, on her eighteenth birthday, and became the lover of both Morning Glory and Wolf. "For me it was yet another romance come true," says Morning Glory. "I was able to have the other man who I love most in my life and the woman I love most in my life be bonded in the same way that Oberon and I were bonded."

Two days after her wedding to Wolf, which was performed by Morning Glory and Oberon, who are legally recognized clergy of the Church of All Worlds, Wynter is weary yet has the serene glow of the newly betrothed. With her red hair, pale, lightly freckled skin, and long loose dress, she has that Celtic goddess look you sometimes see in young women who work in head shops. When we meet in the family's garden, where the wedding ceremony took place, she has just returned from the house of some of her outside lovers, a male/female couple that she sees regularly. She tries to get at least two nights a week with her husband. Every other Wednesday she sleeps with Morning Glory. Wynter has, in current rotation, approximately twenty lovers.

"I never know who I'm sleeping with on Wednesday night because every other Wednesday Wolfie goes gaming," Wynter says. "I always forget what Wednesday it is, so I'm like 'Hmm, who am I sleeping with?' It's amazing that I lead this life because I'm really into my solitary space. I need my time to be alone. Usually I take it in the morning. I take two hours and I go in the hot tub and I read *Harry Potter* and write in my journal. All my nights are filled so every morning I take time and do what I want to do."

We are soon joined by Jon, a tall blue-eyed blond with a long ponytail. Of all the Ravenhearts, he's the "straightest" looking. His clothes suggest no particular cultural affiliation. As a computer specialist, he's also the only Ravenheart who has a job outside the home. Jon fell in love with Liza in 1998 and became an official Ravenheart just this past January. Today he's hanging out with a young woman named Jezebel, who isn't a member of the family but who is living in one of the apartments next to the house. Jon and Jezebel are currently lovers. In the past, Jezebel has been involved in threesomes with Wolf and Wynter. These days she's taking some time for herself, happy to be Jon's "secondary" (his primary being Liza) and learning to be her "own primary."

"When I moved onto this property I had to assure Jon that I wasn't moving in for him," says Jezebel, who, unlike just about everyone else in this story, actually tells me her legal name—Jennifer. "It was just because I wanted to live here."

"Right now I'm being pretty particular about who I sleep with," says Jon. "I don't have a lot of lovers."

Morning Glory, who has ambled into the garden, nods approvingly to Jon and gives him a supportive little thumbs-up. You can't help but wonder if the discernment he's just articulated is the unconscious wish of every Ravenheart.

Jon had heard of the Ravenhearts well before he ever got involved with them. He met Liza through an "erotic community," which she describes as an organized retreat wherein groups of thirty or so people get together and are "openly sexual with each other." Jon was a bit intimidated when he learned that her primary lover was Oberon Ravenheart, not for reasons having to do with sexual prowess, but because Jon feared his knowledge of paganism wasn't sufficiently developed. But the family embraced him wholeheartedly. It also helped that, like Wolf, he was a gamer.

"The first step to becoming a Ravenheart is you have to fall madly in love with someone who already is a Ravenheart and they have to fall madly in love with you," says Liza, who calls Jon "a very special person" for being able to enter such a large, established group. "Then comes the difficult part. Just being madly in love and having some kind of partnership with one of us doesn't make you a Ravenheart. You have to have a relationship with every Ravenheart. In other words, every Ravenheart has to be in harmony with your presence."

It would seem that to become a Ravenheart you'd also have to meet a need that no one else is meeting. The idea that different people fulfill different needs, sexually and otherwise, is an almost constant refrain in the household. In some cases, it's abundantly clear what one person can bring to the table that another can't. "Oberon and Jon are over thirty years apart," says Liza. "Obviously they're totally different. Oberon has a lot of wisdom and experience. Jon is very loving and playful."

"The way I make love to Morning Glory is different than the way I make love to Wynter," says Wolf. "Having to accommodate the needs of different women makes me a better lover. You don't have to be in a poly relationship to understand that people have different needs sexually or whatever. If I were to go down the line and think of how I was sexually with the different women I've dated, being the same with each of them would just not be appropriate."

Wynter, as Wolf describes her, is "catch as catch can." She likes to dress up in sexy clothes and seduce him while he's paying bills. If she's in the garden, she wants to have sex in the garden. She also likes to do it in the hot tub. "If she says 'Let's take a hot tub' it means 'Let's have sex,'" Wolf says.

The issue of privacy is twofold in the Ravenheart household. On one hand, there are plenty of places to be alone. On the other, walking in on someone having sex is not exactly scandal-worthy. "If someone comes up to the hot tub they'll always say 'May I join you?'" explains Wolf. "If you want to be alone you just say so. But there's also no embarrassing social taboo about sex. That dims the voyeuristic thrill."

The same goes for nudity. Wolf points out that, during my visit, the

Ravenhearts have gone out of their way to keep themselves clothed. "When it's hot, Oberon hardly ever wears clothes," he says. "We think nothing of walking around in the yard naked. That's why we have the privacy fence."

With both sex and nudity stripped of their taboos, the Ravenhearts seem to fall back on role-playing.

"Often Morning Glory and I will dress up and play pirate games," Wolf says. "We also play a lot of nurse games."

The fact that Wolf can have spontaneous, hot tub sex with Wynter and preplanned, full-costumed sex with Morning Glory plays right into their central argument for polyamory, which is, essentially, that it takes a village to fill the libido's every need. "In my monogamous marriage, which was very short-lived, the thing that nearly crushed me was that if I didn't meet every single emotional, physical, sexual, psychological, and mental need that person had, that need went unmet," says Wolf. "Here you don't have that. For example, I don't like horses. But Wynter and Morning Glory love horses. Well, they can go horseback riding together and I don't have to."

This is the kind of argument that can elude those of us who aren't poly. It seems to me that anyone with any kind of relationship experience at all knows that their beloved can't be expected to fill every emotional, physical, psychological, mental, and even sexual need. To most of us, that's what friends, colleagues, psychiatrists, and Internet news groups are for.

"Why do I have to live with someone in order to go horseback riding with them?" says Morning Glory. "Because then my wife and I can go home and have great sex!"

Could it be that great sex is what some polys do rather than going out for coffee? When Morning Glory counts the number of lovers she expects to have this year ("People who if I find myself in any kind of proximity to them there's a high probability that sex will occur"), she arrives at a number around twenty. This includes people she might run into occasionally or see when she travels out of town. She thinks about this in a manner that I might apply to how many people I'd expect to have lunch with in a given year.

"By becoming sexually involved with someone I feel like I can make a difference in their life," says Morning Glory. "For years I've found people and it's like I have some kind of calling to help them. It's like the goddess taps me on the shoulder and says 'That one over there.' I've never been a prostitute. I've never charged for my sexual favors. But I have bestowed them generously all over the planet and tried to do so from a place of energizing people and turning them on and getting them involved with being happy in their own lives."

Asking a poly whether or not they get jealous is sort of like asking a tall person how the weather is up there. The question got old a long time ago and to the Ravenhearts it seems irrelevant. According to Oberon, the answer again goes back to Robert A. Heinlein's *Stranger in a Strange Land* concept, which is, as Heinlein wrote, that "love is that condition where another person's happiness is essential to your own." In other words, if you love someone, set them up with someone else. The Ravenhearts often introduce each other to new potential sex partners. It's a kind of mitzvah Liza calls "a conspiracy of heart's desire."

"Whenever we start to talk about poly lifestyles the issue of jealousy comes up," says Liza, who seems somehow less earnest than the other members of the family and has an appealing, self-deprecating laugh. "And that really limits the conversation. Because really jealousy is a response to wanting to get your needs met and clumsily going about doing it. When people have their needs met they don't give a damn about what other people are doing."

Unlike Morning Glory and Oberon, who rejected monogamy as early as elementary school, or Wynter, who was raised by poly parents, Liza grew up idolizing her parents' monogamous marriage. Like many of us, the first time she fell in love she hoped it would last forever. Like just about all of us, it didn't. And although she says she didn't enter polyamory because it seemed like a more realistic choice, she admits that romantic notions of monogamy can set nearly impossible standards for relationships.

"Monogamy in the way that we all fantasize it could be is very rare," Liza says. "Any statistic would bear this out, this is not my perception."

Like Oberon, who laments "conventional society's idea that there's only one way to live and everyone has to be shoehorned into it," Liza wishes that people could be more aware of their choices.

"What I would like to see is a world where people are able to look at their alternatives," she says. "They could view their relationships like a work of art over which they have some measure of creative control rather than be plugged into a few options that are unlikely realistically to fit their real temperament and character."

It would be difficult for anyone with an even moderately progressive sensibility to argue that point. If polyamory was solely concerned with shedding light on relationship options that the mainstream, Judeo-Christian world tends to dismiss as impractical or immoral, I would applaud the Ravenhearts for their magnanimousness and their organizational skills and leave it at that. But for many of the Ravenhearts, especially those who appear to have the most partners, I suspect there is another set of values at work. It has to do with the degree to which they hang their polyamory on their religion and the degree to which that religion is dependent upon the science fiction and fantasy subculture.

When Morning Glory talks about the polyamorous ideas conveyed in Heinlein's novel, her summary goes like this: "He spun a really fascinating possibility. What if you didn't have to stop dating? You could continue including your lovers as your best friends and their lovers as their best friends. You could build a whole social structure of a family that was bonded on this profound spiritual and sexual level."

As nice as this sounds, it seems like a much taller order than even monogamy. For those of us who spend the majority of our time and mental energy wrestling with the conventions and demands of mainstream, heterogeneous society, the notion of becoming best friends with your lovers and their lovers and everyone else who comes down the pike would require suppressing our personal tastes to an almost impossible degree. In other words, most of us aren't capable of liking that many people, let alone bonding with them on a profound spiritual and sexual level.

But here is where I am reminded of the sci-fi kids in high school and the medieval jousters in college and can finally begin to understand exactly why they irked so many of us "normal" people. We didn't like the way it was so easy for them to like each other. We were bothered by the fact that their requirements for being turned on seemed to have less to do with things like culturally sanctioned ideas of attractiveness than with their mutual involvement in the subculture. The Ravenhearts are given to statements like "we connected deeply" and "the human capacity for love is infinite." It's also pretty clear that most of them don't often sleep with anyone who doesn't share their interest in paganism or science fiction, and I can't help but wonder if, in their minds, a deep connection is as close at hand as the next meeting of the Eleusinian Mysteries. By being polyamorous, they are, in effect, giving themselves permission to sleep with other members of the science fiction club. That would seem to call into question just what "infinite capacity for love" really means.

The Ravenhearts's relentless references to things like witchcraft and "the goddess" don't mar the fact that they are fundamentally nice people. Nor does it keep them from being, by all appearances, relatively smart people. Oberon was a leader in the 1960s movement to bring together the various Earth-based religions and unite them under the term "neo-pagan." He is credited with formulating and publishing the theology of deep ecology, best known as the Gaia thesis. All of the Ravenhearts bring some kind of intellectual component to their conversation. They debate various topics. They rationalize their desires. With their deliberate, rather circuitous speech patterns, they sound a lot like philosophy majors at a college with no course requirements.

But like a lot of people immersed in subcultures, there's an intangible gaff in many of the Ravenhearts's perceptions, an imbalance that comes not, as one might assume, from spending more time reading science fiction and fantasy than, say, the newspaper, but from what appears to be a desperate need to compensate for their adolescent nerdiness. Most Ravenhearts talk a lot about feeling alienated in high school. There's much said about being misunderstood. "I wasn't very well socialized," says Morning Glory. "I used to go out into the yard with a flashlight and try to signal the flying saucers to come get me and take me home," Oberon says. "I was a geeky kid," Wolf says. "I didn't lose my virginity until a month before my eighteenth birthday."

Inherent in the belief that one is alienated and "not like the others" is the equally ardent belief that no one anywhere, except perhaps the members of the subculture with which the alienated person has chosen to affiliate himself, has ever had the same feelings. In order to feel truly alienated one must keep a safe distance from the fact that, as self-concepts go, "not like the others" is fairly standard. This distance leads to the kind of mentality that regards the loss of virginity at age eighteen as a freakish thing. It makes a person inclined, as at least two of the Ravenhearts are, to credit the high school drama club—that haven for "misfits" and "outsiders"—with their deliverance into the socialized American teenagerhood. The need to be different means we must constantly promote our unusualness. Oberon tells me he was telepathic until he was two and that he is the reincarnation of his own grandfather. Wolf sometimes bites people.

This is where the Ravenhearts lose me. It's not their polyamory I have a problem with. It's their forced iconoclasm. It's their paraphernalia. It's the fact that they don't seem to sleep with anyone who isn't just like them. The result is that too often "deeply connecting" seems more a matter of shared membership in a subculture—a subculture that is based around the premise of "not fitting in" and has an entire system of toys and tchotchkes and T-shirts to consumerize the idea of not fitting in—than it does with actually connecting.

But despite their heavy involvement in their subculture, the Ravenhearts make a big point of saying that, at root, they're no different from most people. Many polys believe Bill and Hillary Clinton to be polyamorous. "She knows he has other lovers and she ultimately doesn't care," says Wolf. "They're just not in a position to be open about it."

The Ravenhearts pride themselves on their openness. They say they give interviews because they're one of the few poly families who are in a position to be public. Presumably, that position is one of total immersion in the neo-pagan world, a place where, according to them, "diversity is celebrated" and "all forms of relationships and sexual orientations are honored." Here they are immune from the kind of hostility they might elicit if, for instance, they were polyamorous but had names like Steve and Joan and Margaret, and spent their weekends skiing rather than attending the Ancient Ways Festival.

But I would surmise that persecution is not the greatest fear. The greatest fear is of losing the stranger in the strange land. The fear is that "the lifestyle," when it's stripped of its filigrees, will look less like a lifestyle than a human condition, much like being gay or having a tendency to sunburn easily. That's because there's really nothing very strange at all about polyamory. A whole lot of people, in one way or another, participate in it without their friends and neighbors knowing or really caring. The fact that I am interviewing the Ravenhearts and not any of the thousands of other people in this country who probably practice polyamory without knowing there's a name for it says less about our culture's obsession with sex than it does about our obsession with labels. I am interviewing the Ravenhearts because they've given themselves a name, because they have a Web site and a religion and a family business and have decided to incorporate their polyamory into a larger aura of personal style. The Ravenhearts invented a word for this arrangement and have spent the better part of their lives marketing their invention. Ultimately, this story is not about people who have sex with anyone they want. This story is about what happens when you give something a name and, in so doing, deny yourself the unexpected elation that comes from falling in love with someone whose book-shelves hold none of the same books as your own.

AMERICAN SHIKSA

I was born just another blonde. I hunted for Easter eggs. I decorated trees and ate ham. Like all women of the Protestant tradition I was raised to smile, to cooperate and "help out." I made pot holders and read books on cake decorating. I jumped rope and played hopscotch under vast azure skies. But when adolescence struck something strange happened. Instead of becoming a woman, I became a shiksa. I skipped over the typical stuff, the horses and Love's Baby Soft perfume, and went right for the throat. I just didn't have much taste for those praying quarterbacks, those hunks in blue satin choir robes, the hulking social drinkers, the swaggering lifeguards and stockbrokers, the good old boys from the verdant athletic fields of my youth. I discovered Jewish men like I discovered books: in the library, tucked away in the dark corners of suburbia, reticent and wise and spouting out words I had to look up in the dictionary. Unlike Christian men with their innate sense of entitlement, with their height and freckles and stamp collections and summer Dairy Queen jobs, all those homages to the genetics and accoutrements of Western civilization, Jewish men were rife with ambiguity, buzzing with edge. Their sports were cognitive, their affection seemingly cerebral. They were so smart that they managed to convince girls like me that they liked me for my brain, that even though I was a shiksa, even though I had been deprived of Hebrew school and intense dinner debates about the Palestinian Question, I was a smart girl. A Jewish man knows this is the way to get to a woman. A shiksa likes to think that she's intelligent, even though she's bad at math, even though she had to take remedial chemistry with the drug addicts and the pregnant girls. But the Jewish man is cunning in his sensitivity. He zooms in on our insecurities and tells us we're "insightful," that we're "real." He wins because for many of us, insight and reality have always been afterthoughts, the quintessential backseat passengers to that driver blondeness. The evolution from blonde girl to shiksa means discovering the exoticism inherent in her blandness. It is to be a foreigner in an utterly American way.

Herein began a life of loving Jews, of having a crush on the Alex Reiger character on *Taxi*, of preferring Bernstein to Woodward, of deciding that I was naturally neurotic, that angst flattered me, that I was smarter than my blonde counterparts, that I was funnier than my parents, that I was among the "other" chosen. Ten years after I won my first Easter egg hunt, I found myself face-to-face with a grand and brooding destiny, with dark-haired boys who read books and stayed up late, who had circles under their eyes, who looked like wise men, like owls perched on the highest rungs of the evolutionary ladder. These were the boys who, in college, combined their pot with wheat germ, who lent you their paperback of the *Kama Sutra* but asked you not to break the binding. Indeed, this is the allure of the Jewish man: His deviance is too self-conscious to be dangerous. He's a scoundrel but he won't kill you on his motorcycle. He's a molester but not a drunk, a pervert but not a thug.

The first symptom of this infatuation was a desire to be an actual Jew. I yearned for a richer culture, for better debating skills and hair with personality. I was jealous of my Jewish female friends, who never needed to use hot rollers and seemed to know every single person on the East Coast. But my fantasy that I would one morning waking up a Jew soon faded. Even if I converted, the roots were too deep, the culture too personal. Besides, I'm an agnostic, which is a trait only acceptable in natural-born Jews. So I decided that if I couldn't be Jewish I might as well be un-Jewish in as obstreperous and maddening a way as possible. I decided to promote myself by advertising all that I was not. And that meant surrounding myself with Jews and being a gentile. Blonde. Flaky. Adoring.

I soon decided it was my fate—my responsibility, in fact—to surround myself with Jews and eventually marry a Jewish man. I owed it to myself, and even more intensely I owed it to my ancestors, who, in my imagination, had toiled in cultural mediocrity for years, laboring in midwestern farmlands, developing tractor tans, feeding castor oil to cussing kids, shooting rifles straight into the air when there was nothing on TV, doing all those things that are so conspicuously not Jewish.

The dirty secret of goyim everywhere, even those from the highest circles of what the Ralph Lauren home collection would be if it hadn't been the brainchild of a Jew, is that deep inside we're all white trash. Even those who hide behind the cultural cachet of Catholicism or WASPdom know that the distance between Jackie Kennedy and Tonya Harding is just a few rungs on a very rickety ladder. With or without country homes in Kennebunkport or Squibnocket, we're all descendants of shotgun culture, of Coke at breakfast, Triscuits for lunch, 4-H champions, horse thieves, and drunks passed out in front of *60 Minutes*. I myself am the daughter of a former Miss Congeniality. Cuckoo clocks have played a role in my childhood. Tornadoes have been of legitimate concern. I am an American. And we in America know about Jews. We know what we want.

One of the first Jewish men I knew had asked his previous girlfriend to perform fellatio on him while he was driving, but since, being Jewish, he also feared getting into an accident, he suggested that they do this while cruising at fifteen miles per hour around an empty parking lot. During my tenure, I was asked to read aloud from *Portnoy's Complaint* during a car trip from New York to Boston (this he could handle at sixty-five mph). I had never read the book. I had, in fact, confused it somehow with *Roger's Version* and as my lips passed over the pages I wondered when we were going to get to the part about Jesus Christ.

This boy was smart and adorable, a chronic allergy sufferer from Brighton Beach, Brooklyn. He spoke a broken Yiddish. He carried an inhaler of Proventil with him at all times. I was not his girlfriend, merely his backdoor shiksa, a role which suited me fine as I was not interested in full-time motherhood, merely the maid service for which shiksas are so well-known (and well tipped). He told me about his other girlfriends, shiksas of all varieties—black, Asian, Mennonite—whom he invited as guests for Passover seders, after which he would take them to Coney Island and screw them on the sand. I would nod and laugh, even saying "That's interesting," a phrase used often by shiksas when they can't keep up with the conversation. Unlike the Jewish woman, the shiksa is the consummate "other woman." She knows she's not the only one and until she closes the deal by marrying him (extra points for church weddings, even Unitarian), she doesn't care. Her role is not to judge but to conspire, not to bitch but merely moan. Unlike the Jewish woman, who's been raised to have a modicum of pride and certainly wouldn't ruin her hair by doing it on a schmutzy beach, the shiksa probably has sand in her hair anyway.

Ask the Jewish man why he loves the shiksa and the same words always come to his above-average mind: "pliant," "gentle," "breezy." The shiksa is famous for her infinitely bearable lightness. She doesn't boss around handymen. She doesn't talk about her shrink. She doesn't complain about the food in restaurants—she can't tell the difference anyway, having grown up on Green Giant creamed corn. Her primary pose is an embarrassed hand-on-mouth. "Oh, I can't believe I said that," she says without saying anything. Indeed, she often says nothing, which doesn't mean that she has nothing to say, merely that she chooses not to say it. The most brilliant shiksas consider their brains in the same light that they consider their outfits; the old adage "get completely dressed, then take off one piece of jewelry" also applies to the art of conversation. So, she will conjure quite a number of thoughts and offer up only a few, one of which is commonly "Another gin and tonic, please." Like a squirrel gathering acorns she doesn't blow her wad. She lets her Jewish man do most of the talking, thereby securing her position as his number-one dream lay.

Ask us shiksas why we love the Jew and we can come up with at least three reasons but will only dole out two of them: "on time," and "less likely to have a criminal record." The thing we thought but did not say is that other than a professional athlete or a movie star, a Jewish man is the closest a woman can come to having a trophy. To date a Jewish man is to tease him away from his tribe for a while. To marry a Jewish man is to get him to turn his back on the essence of his entire existence—his bar mitzvah photos, his SAT scores, his mother. It is to get him to admit that he loves us so much that he'll trade in scholarship for marshmallow fluff, substitute the Torah for a spanking new set of World Book Encyclopedias. In exchange he can mouth off all he wants and we won't interrupt him. The dynamic between shiksas and the Jewish men who love them is that of dolphin to marine biologist. His intelligence is solid and studied. He's walking rigor. He's done the work. We, on the other hand, have remarkable reasoning powers but prefer to squeak. We splash around in the water. We enjoy balancing things on our noses. (I myself can hang a spoon off my nose.) We're the attraction, the on-air talent. He's the writer/producer/director. We're Kate Capshaw. He's Steven Spielberg—after he's dumped Amy Irving (not our fault).

Another of my Jewish boyfriends proclaimed my lack of Jewishness as proudly as he once sang "Hatikvah" in Hebrew school. His affection spewed out in torrents as if he were an open hydrant. He was kind and reliable and only ordered Cokes in bars. He told me the meanings of words. He filled me in on current events. He cooperated when I insisted that we see both *Beethoven* and *Free Willy* movies the day they opened in theaters. When we rented *Schindler's List* he patiently stopped the tape to explain to me what was happening. He professed his love to me on a daily basis. He loved my shiksadom, and insisted that his family could learn to love it too. Despite being expected to call them almost daily, he claimed to have "a very mature relationship" with his parents, one in which their parental love subsumed their dismay at his taste for shiksas and they accepted him, as parents accept a retarded child, for who he was.

This claim did not prevent him from, inexplicably, loving me with considerably less verve during weekends when he took me home for family visits. Within hours of our arrival he would suddenly contract a case of food, sun, or allergy medicine poisoning and be forced to go upstairs and lie down, leaving me to fend for myself. Little did he know that while he slept, knocked out on Benadryl or burned by the fierce Jersey shore sun, his parents schemed against him. For this is the scenario in which all Jewish parents, having apparently attended the same lecture at the synagogue called "Booting the Blonde: How to Get that Shiksa Out of Your Precious, Brilliant Son's Life for Good," behave identically. This is when they get out the photographs of trips to Israel and make a big deal about recent editorial changes in *The Jewish Weekly.* This is when they get out IRA portfolios and pore over them as if they were the original manuscript of *Ulysses.* They show the shiksa photographs from their son's bar mitzvah, cleverly trying to drive her away by showing her what a dork he looked like in a yarmulke. They talk about what an ugly baby he was, hoping to discourage her from producing equally hideous offspring. They unabashedly discuss bodily functions, cruelly alienating the shiksa because they all know that her family doesn't have bodily functions. At this the shiksa can merely sit there and say "That's interesting," all the while dreaming of a juicy hunk of Boar's Head.

I've dated some non-Jews, men whose chief bodily functions involved the passage of Scotch down the esophagus, men who haven't noticed that they still have a poster of Wayne Gretsky on their wall. I went on a date with a Protestant from Minnesota who told me he dropped out of library science school "because it was too stressful." I went on a date with a lapsed Catholic who got up to use the men's room and passed out on the floor. He later explained that he'd "had a few cocktails in the hours preceding our date." It turned out this was eight hours and these cocktails were the sort rarely if ever consumed by Jewish men. Blue drinks. Drinks with swizzle sticks shaped like monkeys.

"The Monkey looks like a child trying to master a multiplication problem," Portnoy intoned. "But not a dumb child, Not stupid at all!" This is not the swizzle stick monkey but the shiksa, whose desire for the Jewish man to think she's smart is equal to the Jewish woman's desire to hear him say, "Funny, you don't look Jewish." The appearance of a raw braininess is the shiksa's ultimate goal, the final frontier of "otherness" as it manifests in her so un-other world. The shiksa needs the Jewish man because without him she cannot exist. Without him she is just another blonde girl. And the shiksa is blonde even when she isn't blonde. Imposed on her world is a perpetual weary sunshine, gleaming rays reflected from Christ's own well-flossed teeth. Yellow light surrounds her; she seems bathed in Parkay margarine. She has much to overcome. She must do her homework. She must try to get through at least some of the *New York Times* front section before turning to the Style section. She must subtly manipulate her Jewish man into eating an occasional Cheez Whiz treat, into buying a Christmas tree. She must avoid being stabbed by Norman Mailer. She must avoid engaging women like Susan Sontag in philosophical debate—at this, as in arguments with any Barnard graduate, the shiksa will lose. The shiksa simply must know her place at the seder table. She must help clean up afterwards. She must try to stay sober. She must send the kids to Hebrew school as long as they also twirl the baton. Moreover she must learn to pronounce *charoset* as well as eat it. It tastes like an hors d'oeuvre in purgatory, but she'll suffer. Yes, she'll suffer, too.

MUSIC IS MY BAG

The image I want to get across is that of the fifteen-year-old boy with the beginning traces of a mustache who hangs out in the band room after school playing the opening bars of a Billy Joel song on the piano. This is the kid who, in the interests of adopting some semblance of personal style, wears a fedora hat and a scarf with a black-and-white design of a piano keyboard. This is the kid who, in addition to having taught himself some tunes from the *Songs from the Attic* sheet music he bought at the local Sam Ash, probably also plays the trombone in the marching band, and experienced a seminal moment one afternoon as he vaguely flirted with a not-yet-kissed, clarinet-playing girl, a girl who is none too popular but whose propensity for leaning on the piano as the boy plays the opening chords of "Captain Jack" give him a clue as to the social possibilities that might be afforded him via the marching band.

If the clarinet-playing girl is an average student musician, she carries her plastic Selmer in the standard-issue black plastic case. If she has demonstrated any kind of proficiency, she carries her Selmer in a tote bag that reads "Music Is My Bag." The boy in the piano-key scarf definitely has music as his bag. He may not yet have the tote bag, but the hat, the Billy Joel, the tacit euphoria brought on by a sexual awakening that, for him, centers entirely around band, is all he needs to be delivered into the unmistakable realm that is Music Is My Bagdom.

I grew up in Music Is My Bag culture. The walls of my parents' house were covered with framed art posters from musical events: The San Francisco Symphony's 1982 production of *St. Matthew's Passion*, The Metropolitan Opera's 1976 production of *Aida*, the original Broadway production of *Sweeney Todd*. Ninety percent of the books on the shelves were about music, if not actual musical scores. Childhood ceramics projects made by my brother and me were painted with eighth notes and treble clef signs. We owned a deck of cards with portraits of the great composers on the back. A baby grand piano overtook the room that would have been the dining room if my parents hadn't forgone a table and renamed it "the music room." This room also contained an imposing hi-fi system and a $300 wooden music stand. Music played at all times: Brahms, Mendelssohn, cast recordings of Sondheim musicals, a cappella Christmas albums. When my father sat down with a book, he read musical scores, humming quietly and tapping his foot. When I was ten, my mother decided we needed to implement a before-dinner ritual akin to saying grace, so she composed a short song, asking us all to contribute a lyric, and we held hands and sang it before eating. My lyric was, "There's a smile on our face and it seems to say all the wonderful things we've all done today." My mother insisted on harmonizing at the end. She also did this when singing "Happy Birthday."

Harmonizing on songs like "Happy Birthday" is a clear indication of the Music Is My Bag personality. If one does not have an actual bag that reads "Music Is My Bag"—as did the violist in the chamber music trio my mother set up with some women from the Unitarian Church—a $300 music stand and musical-note coasters will more than suffice. To avoid confusion, let me also say that there are many different Bags in life. Some friends of my parents have a $300 dictionary stand, a collection of silver bookmarks, and once threw a dinner party wherein the guests had to dress up as members of the Bloomsbury Group. These people are Literature Is My Bag. I know people who are Movies Are My Bag (detectable by key chains shaped like projectors, outdated copies of *Halliwell's Film Guide*, and one too many T-shirts from things like the San Jose Film Festival), people who are Cats Are My Bag (self-explanatory), and, perhaps most annoyingly, Where I Went To College Is My Bag (Yale running shorts, plastic Yale tumblers, Yale Platinum Plus MasterCard, and, yes, even Yale screensavers—all this in someone aged forty or more, the perennial contributor to the class notes).

Having a Bag connotes the state of being overly interested in something, and yet, in a certain way, not interested enough. It has a hobbyish quality to it, a sense that the enthusiasm developed at a time when the enthusiast was lacking in some significant area of social or intellectual life. Music Is My Bag is the mother of all Bags, not just because in the early 1980s some consumer force of the public radio fund-drive variety distributed a line of tote bags that displayed that slogan, but because its adherents, or, as they tend to call themselves, "music lovers," give off an aura that distinguishes them from the rest of the population. It's an aura that has to do with a sort of benign cluelessness, a condition that, even in middle age, smacks of that phase between prepubescence and real adolescence. Music Is My Bag people have a sexlessness to them. There is a pastiness to them. They can never seem to find a good pair of jeans. You can spot them on the street, the female French horn player in concert dress hailing a cab to Lincoln Center around seven o'clock in the evening, her earrings too big, her hairstyle unchanged since 1986.

The fifty-something recording engineer with the running shoes and the shoulder bag. The Indiana marching band kids in town for the Macy's Thanksgiving Day Parade, snapping photos of each other in front of the Hard Rock Cafe, having sung their parts from the band arrangement of *Hello Dolly* the whole way on the bus, thinking, *knowing*, that it won't get better than this. Like all Music Is My Bag people, they are a little too in love with the trappings. They know what their boundaries are and load up their allotted space with memorabilia, saving the certificates of participation from regional festivals, the composer-a-month calendars, the Mostly Mozart posters. Their sincerity trumps attempts at snideness. The boys' sarcasm only goes a fraction of the way there, the girls will never be great seducers. They grow up to look like high school band directors even if they're not. They give their pets names like Wolfgang and Gershwin. Their hemlines are never quite right.

I played the oboe. This is not an instrument to be taken lightly. The oboist runs a high risk of veering into Music Is My Bag culture, mostly because to get beyond the entry level is to give oneself over to an absorption with technique that can make a person vulnerable to certain vagaries of a subcategory, the oboe phylum. This inevitably leads to the genus of *wind ensemble* culture, which concerns itself with the sociopolitical infrastructure of the woodwind section, the disproportionate number of solo passages, a narcissistic pride in sounding the A that tunes the orchestra. Not many people play the oboe. It's a difficult instrument, beautiful when played well, horrifying when played poorly. I was self-conscious about playing the oboe, mostly because so many people confuse it with the bassoon, its much larger, ganglier cousin in the double-reed family. The act of playing the oboe, unlike the graceful arm positions of the flute or the violin, is not a photogenic one. The embouchure puckers the face into a grimace; my childhood and adolescence is documented by photos that make me look slightly deformed—the lipless girl. It's not an instrument for the vain. Oboe playing revolves almost entirely around saliva. Spit gets caught in the keys and the joints and must be blown out using cigarette rolling paper as a blotter (a scandalous drugstore purchase for a twelve-year-old). Spit can accumulate on the floor if you play for too long. Spit must constantly be sucked out from both sides of the reed. The fragile, temperamental reed is the player's chronic medical condition. It must be tended to constantly. It must be wet but never too wet, hard enough to emit a decent sound, but soft enough to blow air through. The oboist must never stray far from moisture; the reed is forever in her mouth, in a paper cup of water that teeters on the music stand, being doused at a drinking fountain in Parsippany High School at the North Jersey Regional Band and Orchestra Audition. After a certain age, the student oboist must learn to make her own reeds, build them from bamboo using knives and shavers. Most people don't realize this. Reed-making is an eighteenth-century exercise, something that would seem to require an apprenticeship before undertaking solo. But oboists, occupying a firm, albeit wet, patch of ground under the tattered umbrella of Music Is My Bag, never quite live in the same era as everyone else.

Though I did, at one point, hold the title of second-best high school player in the state of New Jersey, I was a mediocre oboist. My discipline was lacking, my enthusiasm virtually nil, and my comprehension of rhythm (in keeping with a lifelong math phobia) held me back considerably. But being without an aptitude for music was, in my family, tantamount to being a Kennedy who knows nothing of politics. Aptitude was something, perhaps even the only thing, I possessed. As indifferent to the oboe as I was—and I once began an orchestra rehearsal without noticing that I had neglected to screw the bell, which is the entire bottom portion, onto the rest of my instrument—I managed to be good enough to play in the New Jersey All State High School Orchestra as well as a local adult symphony. I even gained acceptance into a music conservatory. These aren't staggering accomplishments unless you consider the fact that I rarely practiced. If I had practiced with any amount of regularity, I could have been, as my parents would have liked me to be, one of those kids who was schlepped to Juilliard on Saturdays. If I had practiced slightly more than that, I could have gone to Juilliard for college. If I had practiced a lot I could have ended up in the New York Philharmonic. This is not an exaggeration, merely a moot point. I didn't practice. I haven't picked up the oboe since my junior year in college, where, incidentally, I sat first chair in the orchestra even though I did not practice once the entire time.

I never practiced and yet I always practiced. My memory is always of being unprepared, yet I was forced to sit in the chair for so many hours that I suspect something else must have been at work, a lack of consciousness about it, an inability to practice on my own. "Practice" was probably among the top five words spoken in our family, the other four probably being the names of our family members. Today, almost ten years since I've practiced, the word has lost the resonance of our usage. I now think of practice in terms of law or medicine. There is a television show called *The Practice*, and it seems odd to me that I never associate the word sprawled across the screen with the word that wove relentlessly throughout our family discourse. For my entire childhood and adolescence, practicing was an ongoing condition. It was both a given and a punishment. When we were bad, we practiced. When we were idle, we practiced. Before dinner and TV and friends coming over and bedtime and a thousand other things that beckoned with the possibility of taking place without all that harrowing noise, we practiced. "You have practicing and homework," my mother said every day. In that order. My father said the same thing without the homework part.

Much of the reason I could never quite get with the oboe-playing program was that I developed, at a very young age, a deep contempt for the Music Is My Bag world. Instead of religion, my family had music, and it was the church against which I rebelled. I had clergy for parents. My father: professional composer and arranger, keyboard player and trombonist, brother of a high school band director in Illinois. My mother: pianist and music educator of the high school production of *Carousel* genre. My own brother a reluctant Christ figure. A typically restless second child in youth (he quit piano lessons but later discovered he could play entirely by ear), my brother recently completed the final mix of a demo CD of songs he wrote and performed—mid-eighties pop, late Doobie Brothers groove. His Los Angeles house is littered with Billy Joel and Bruce Hornsby sheet music, back issues of *Stereo Review*, the liner notes to the digital remastering of John Williams's score for *Star Wars*. Music is the Bag.

I compose songs in my sleep. I can't do it awake. I'll dream of songwriters singing onstage. I'll hear them perform new songs, songs I've never heard, songs I therefore must have written. In childhood I never put one thought toward composing a song. It would have been like composing air, creating more of something of which there was already quite enough. Wind players like flutists and saxophonists need as much air as they can get. Oboists are always trying to get rid of air. They calibrate what they need to get the reed to vibrate, end up using even less, and dispense with the rest out the corners of their mouths. It's all about exhaling. On an eighth rest, they're as likely to blow air out as they are to steal a breath. There's always too much air for oboists, too much of everything, too many bars when they're not playing and too many bars where there's hardly anyone playing but them, too many percussion players dropping triangles on the floor, too many violinists playing "Eleanor Rigby" before the rehearsal starts. Orchestras have only two oboists, first chair and second chair, pilot and copilot, though the "co" in this case is, like all "co's," a misnomer. The second oboist is the perpetual backup system, the one on call, the one who jumps in and saves the other when his reed dries up in the middle of a solo, when he misses his cue, when he freezes in panic before trying to hit a high D. I've been first oboist and I've been second oboist and, let me tell you, first is better, but not by much. It's still the oboe. Unlike the gregarious violinist or the congenial cellist, the oboist is a lone wolf. To play the oboe in an orchestra is to complete an obstacle course of solos and duets with the first flutist who, if she is hard-core Music Is My Bag, will refer to herself as a "floutist." Oboe solos dot the great symphonies like land mines, the pizzicati that precede them are drumrolls, the conductor's pointing finger an arrow for the whole audience to see: Here comes the oboe, two bars until the oboe, now, *now*. It's got to be nailed, one flubbed arpeggio, one flat half note, one misplaced pinky in the middle of a run of sixteenth notes, and everyone will hear, *everyone*.

My parents' presence at a high school orchestra concert turned what should have been a routine event into something akin to the finals of the Olympic women's figure skating long program. Even from the blinding, floodlit stage I could practically see them in the audience, clucking at every error, grimacing at anything even slightly out of tune. Afterwards, when the other parents—musically illiterate chumps—were patting their kids on the head and loading the tuba into the station wagon, I would receive my critique. "You were hesitating in the second movement of the Haydn Variations." "You over-anticipated in the berceuse section of the Stravinsky." "Your tone was excellent in the first movement but then your chops ran out." My brother, who was forced for a number of years to play the French horn, was reduced to a screaming fight with our father in the school parking lot, the kind of fight only possible between fathers and sons. He'd bumbled too many notes, played out of tune, committed some treasonous infraction against the family reputation. My father gave him the business on the way out to the car, eliciting the alto curses of a fourteen-year-old, pages of music everywhere, an instrument case slammed on the pavement.

This sort of rebellion was not my style. I cried instead. I cried in the seventh grade when the letter telling me I'd been accepted to the North Jersey regional orchestra arrived three days late. I cried in the tenth grade, when I ended up in the All State Band instead of the orchestra. I cried when I thought I'd given a poor recital (never mind that the audience thought I was brilliant—all morons), cried before lessons (underprepared), cried after lessons (sentenced to a week of reviewing the loathsome F-sharp étude). Mostly I cried during practice drills supervised by my father. These were torture sessions wherein some innocent tooting would send my father racing downstairs from his attic study, screaming "Count, count, you're not *counting*! Jesus Christ!" Out would come a pencil—if not an actual conductor's baton—hitting the music stand, forcing me to repeat the tricky fingerings again and again, speeding up the tempo so I'd be sure to hit each note when we took it back down to real time. These sessions would last for hours, my mouth muscles shaking from atrophy, tears welling up from fatigue and exasperation. If we had a copy of the piano part, my mother would play the accompaniment, and together my parents would bark commands. "Articulate the eighth notes more. More staccato on the tonguing. Don't tap your foot, tap your toe inside your shoe." The postman heard a lot of this. The neighbors heard all of it. After practicing we'd eat dinner, but not before that song—"There's a smile on our face, and it seems to say all the wonderful things . . . " "Good practice session today," my mother would say, dishing out the casserole, WQXR's *Symphony Hall* playing over the kitchen speakers. "Yup, sounding pretty good," my father would say. "How about one more go at it before bed?"

My mother called my oboe a "horn." This infuriated me. "Do you have your horn?" she'd ask every single morning. "Do you need your horn for school today?" She maintained that this terminology was technically correct, that among musicians, a "horn" was anything into which air was blown. My oboe was a $4,000 instrument, high-grade black grenadilla with sterling silver keys. It was no horn. But such semantics are a staple of Music Is My Bag, the overfamiliar stance that reveals a desperate need for subcultural affiliation, the musical equivalent of people in the magazine business who refer to publications like *Glamour* and *Forbes* as "books." As is indicated by the use of "horn," there's a subtly macho quality to Music Is My Bag. The persistent insecurity of musicians, especially classical musicians, fosters a kind of jargon that would be better confined to the military or major league baseball. Cellists talk about rock stops and rosin as though they were comparing canteen belts or brands of glove grease. They have their in-jokes and aphorisms, "The rock stops here," "Eliminate Violins In Our Schools."

I grew up surrounded by phrases like "rattle off that solo," "nail that lick," and "build up your chops." Like acid-washed jeans, "chops" is a word that should only be invoked by rock and roll guitarists but is more often uttered with the flailing, badly timed anti-authority of the high school clarinet player. Like the violinist who plays "Eleanor Rigby" before rehearsal, the clarinet player's relationship to rock and roll maintains its distance. Rock and roll is about sex. It is something unloved by parents and therefore unloved by Music Is My Bag people, who make a vocation of pleasing their parents, of studying trig and volunteering at the hospital and making a run for the student government even though they're well aware they have no chance of winning. Rock and roll is careless and unstudied. It might possibly involve drinking. It most certainly involves dancing. It flies in the face of the central identity of Music Is My Baggers, who chose as their role models those painfully introverted characters from young adult novels—"the klutz," "the bookworm," "the late bloomer." When given a classroom assignment to write about someone who inspires her, Music Is My Bag will write about her grandfather or perhaps Jean-Pierre Rampaul. If the bad-attitude kid in the back row writes about AC/DC's Angus Young, Music Is My Bag will believe in her heart that this student should receive a failing grade. Rock and roll is not, as her parents would say when the junior high drama club puts on a production of *Grease*, "appropriate for this age group." Even in the throes of adolescence, Music Is My Bag will deny adolescence. Even at age sixteen, she will hold her ears when the rock and roll gets loud, saying it ruins her sense of overtones, saying she has sensitive ears. Like a retiree, she will classify the whole genre as nothing but a bunch of noise, though it is likely she is a fan of Yes.

During the years that I was a member of the New Jersey All State Orchestra I would carpool to rehearsals with the four or so other kids from my town who made All State every year. This involved spending as much as two hours each way in station wagons driven by people's parents and, inevitably, the issue would arise of what music would be played in the car. Among the most talented musicians in school was a freshman who, in addition to being hired by the Boston Symphony Orchestra at age twenty-two, possessed, as a fifteen-year-old, a ripe enthusiasm for the singer Amy Grant. This was back in the mid-1980s when Amy Grant's hits were still relegated to the Christian charts. Our flute-playing carpool-mate loved Amy Grant. Next to Prokofiev and the Hindemith Flute Sonata, Amy Grant occupied the number-one spot in this girl's studious, late-blooming heart. Since her mother, like many parents of Baggers, was devoted solely to her daughter's musical and academic career, she did most of the driving to these boony spots— Upper Chatham High School, Monmouth Regional, Long Branch Middle School. Mile after New Jersey Turnpike mile, we were serenaded by the wholesome synthesizers of songs like "Saved By Love" and "Wait for the Healing," only to spill out of the car and take no small relief in the sound of twenty-five of New Jersey's best student violinists playing "Eleanor Rigby" before the six-hour rehearsal.

To participate in a six-hour rehearsal of the New Jersey All State Band or Orchestra is to enter a world so permeated by Music Is My Bagdom that it becomes possible to confuse the subculture with an entire species, as if Baggers, like lobsters or ferns, require special conditions in order to thrive. Their ecosystem is the auditorium and the adjacent band room, any space that makes use of risers. To eat lunch and dinner in these venues is to see the accessories of Badgom tumble from purses, knapsacks, and totes; here more than anyplace are the real McCoys, actual Music Is My Bag *bags*, canvas satchels filled with stereo Walkmen and A.P. math homework and Trapper Keeper notebooks featuring the piano-playing Schroeder from the *Peanuts* comic strip. The dinner break is when I would embark on oboe maintenance, putting the reed in water, swabbing the instrument dry, removing the wads of wax that, during my orthodontic years, I placed over my front teeth to keep the inside of my mouth from bleeding. Just as I had hated the entropy of recess back in my grade-school years, I loathed the dinner breaks at All State rehearsals. To maximize rehearsal time, the wind section often ate separately from the strings, which left me alone with the band types. They'd wolf down their sandwiches and commence with their jam session, a cacophonous white noise of scales, finger exercises, and memorized excerpts from their hometown marching band numbers. During these dinner breaks I'd generally hang with the other oboist. For some reason, this was almost always a tall girl who wore sneakers with corduroy pants and a turtleneck with nothing over it. This is fairly typical Music Is My Bag garb, though oboists have a particular spin on it, a spin characterized more than anything by lack of spin. Given the absence in most classical musicians of a style gene, this is probably a good thing. Oboists don't accessorize. They don't wear buttons on their jackets that say "Oboe Power" or "Who Are You Going to Tune To?"

There's high-end Bagdom and low-end Bagdom, with a lot of room in between. Despite my parents' paramilitary practice regimes, I have to give them credit for being fairly high-end Baggers. There were no piano-key scarves in our house, no "World's Greatest Trombonist" figurines, no plastic tumblers left over from my father's days as director of the Stanford University Marching Band. Such accessories are the mandate of the lowest tier of Music Is My Bag, a stratum whose mascot is P.D.Q. Bach, whose theme song is "Piano Man," and whose regional representative is the kid in high school who plays not only the trumpet but the piano, saxophone, flute, string bass, accordion, and wood block. This kid, considered a wunderkind by his parents and the rest of the band community, plays none of these instruments well, but the fact that he knows so many different sets of fingerings, the fact that he has the potential to earn some college money by performing as a one-man band at the annual state teacher's conference, makes him a hometown hero. He may not be a football player. He may not even gain access to the Ivy League. But in the realm of Music Is My Bag, the kid who plays every instrument, particularly when he can play Billy Joel songs on every instrument, is the Alpha Male.

The flip side of the one-man-band kid are those Music Is My Baggers who are not musicians at all. These are the kids who twirl flags or rifles in the marching band, kids who blast music in their rooms and play not air guitar but air keyboards, their hands fluttering out in front of them, the hand positions not nearly as important as the attendant head motions. This is the essence of Bagdom. It is to take greater pleasure in the reverb than the melody, to love the lunch break more than the rehearsal, the rehearsal more than the performance, the clarinet case more than the clarinet. It is to think nothing of sending away for the deluxe packet of limited-edition memorabilia that is being sold for the low, low price of one's entire personality. It is to let the trinkets do the talking.

I was twenty-one when I stopped playing the oboe. I wish I could come up with a big, dramatic reason why. I wish I could say that I sustained some kind of injury that prevented me from playing (it's hard to imagine what kind of injury could sideline an oboist—a lip strain? Carpal tunnel?) or that I was forced to sell my oboe in order to help a family member in crisis or, better yet, that I suffered a violent attack in which my oboe was used as a weapon against me before being stolen and melted down for artillery. But the truth, I'm ashamed to say, has more to do with what in college I considered to be an exceptionally long walk from my dormitory to the music building, and the fact that I was wrapped up in a lot of stuff that, from my perspective at the time, precluded the nailing of Rachmaninoff licks. Without the prodding of my parents or the structure of a state-run music education program, my oboe career had to run on self-motivation alone—not an abundant resource—and when my senior year started I neither registered for private lessons nor signed up for the orchestra, dodging countless calls from the director imploring me to reassume my chair.

Since then, I haven't set foot in a rehearsal room, put together a folding music stand, fussed with a reed, marked up music, practiced scales, tuned an orchestra or performed any of the countless activities that had dominated my existence up until that point. There are moments every now and then when I'll hear the oboe-dominated tenth movement of the Bach *Mass in B Minor* or the berceuse section of Stravinsky's *Firebird* and long to find a workable reed and pick up the instrument again. But then I imagine how terrible I'll sound after eight dormant years and put the whole idea out of my mind before I start to feel sad about it. I can still smell the musty odor of the inside of my oboe case, the old-ladyish whiff of the velvet lining and the tubes of cork grease and the damp fabric of the key pads. Unlike the computer on which I now work, my oboe had the sense of being an ancient thing. Brittle and creaky, it was vulnerable when handled by strangers. It needed to be packed up tight, dried out in just the right places, kept away from the heat and the cold and from anyone too stupid to confuse it with a clarinet.

What I really miss about the oboe is having my hands on it. I could come at that instrument from any direction or any angle and know every indentation on every key, every spot that leaked air, every nick on every square inch of wood. When enough years go by, the corporeal qualities of an instrument become as familiar to its player as, I imagine, those of a long-standing lover. Knowing precisely how the weight of the oboe was distributed between my right thumb and left wrist, knowing, above all, that the weight would feel the same way every time, every day, for every year that I played, was a feeling akin to having ten years of knowledge about the curve of someone's back. Since I stopped playing the oboe, I haven't had the privilege of that kind of familiarity. That's not an exaggeration, merely a moot point.

VARIATIONS ON GRIEF

Several years ago, my oldest friend died, presenting me with an occasion not to be sad, not to cry, not to tell people and have them not know how to respond. Several years ago, I decided to create an ironic occurrence rather than a tragedy, a cautionary tale rather than the wretched injustice it really was. This is a neat trick, this business of utter detachment from everything less than great that goes on, this position of being perched on a cartoon drawing of a crescent moon, looking down at all the lonely people, all the stupid ones with their souls so foolishly close to the linings of their coats.

What my friend did was catch a virus from the air. This is true. This is, in fact, the only aspect of the event that remains unequivocal. I now suspect it was hantavirus—the strain that is passed along from even the most remote contact with rodents—but there was never any concrete evidence of this. Like a tuft of dandelion seed, this virus wafted into Brian Peterson's body as he walked down the street or sat by a window or perhaps even slept in the bed he'd purchased from Jensen-Lewis, the bed with the Ralph Lauren sheets for which he'd fastidiously shopped at Bloomingdales—"fabric for living." Except that he died. All but dropped dead. Unlike an encounter with a dandelion seed, contact with such a virus is a one-in-eight-million chance. Four to six people each year die of this. One stands in greater risk of being abducted by a celebrated criminal, or of being visited by the Publisher's Clearing House Prize Patrol, or of standing on the precise acre of land where a jetliner falls after the failure of a hydraulics system. This is the sort of chance that, upon impact, transcends itself and becomes something closer to fate.

Brian is someone who accomplished nothing in his life other than his death. This is an ugly admission, a brutal interpretation of facts I have not been able to process any other way. He died at twenty-two. Very few people came to his funeral. There were only a handful of friends to call, vague acquaintances who had faded into the murk of adulthood, who had disappeared down roads of maturity that always appeared to Brian as hazy and not worth the trip. His life had been a string of failures: an unremarkable education in suburban public schools, an abandoned college career, a less than half-hearted attempt to become a writer. He was an only child, spoiled by parents who had no friends and furnished him with an expensive car and expensive clothes that he drove and wore no particular place. His audience was himself, a reflexive relationship that resulted in unbearably empty spaces for both parties. This was a life bereft of even tragedy, until he finally fixed that. He let death come to him—although that, of course, is a matter of interpretation, as is every component of the existence and lack of existence of Brian Peterson.

I liked Brian because he liked me, because he laughed at my jokes, let me drive his car, and complimented my appearance even when I'd done something atrocious to my hair. I liked him because he didn't hold me in contempt for refusing to reciprocate the romantic aspects of his affection for me. He let me talk about other men. He let me watch whatever I wanted on his TV, even if it was *National Geographic* specials about the spotted leopard of Ghana. I liked Brian because he had nothing to do with the passage of time. He was immune to maturity, resistant to forward motion. He existed the way childhood homes are supposed to and never do, as a foundation that never shifts, a household that never gets new wallpaper, or turns your bedroom into a study, or is sold in exchange for a condo in Florida.

When he left this planet, he left me and very few others, and if those Christian alternatives to life really exist, then he must know by now that we will never be reunited. If those opposable H's are true, then he is in Heaven for never committing any crime, and I'll find myself in Hell one day for the spin that I have put on his death. My spin is this: I believe that he couldn't do anything other than die. None of us who grew up with him could imagine an alternative. And the fact that he didn't officially kill himself was enough to make all of us believe in the supernatural, or at least some kind of devilish warden hovering over our lives, whispering in our waxy ears, "Do something, or die."

Some specifics: Over the New Year's weekend of 1993, Brian came down with the flu. He called in some antibiotics and took a few. Then he left the cigarettes on the kitchen table, lay down in bed, and never got up. Also on the table was the December 22 edition of the *New York Post*, the January issue of *Esquire*, and a copy of *TV Guide* already cracked at the spine. He was a person who planned his television watching as if the programs were activities written in a Filofax, as if they were the contents of his life, which they, in fact, were. They were standing appointments, not even penciled in.

On January 4, Brian's mother called me. I was eating a bagel. I answered on the third ring; somehow I remember this. She told me he was in the hospital, that he had lain in bed in his apartment for six days until she and his father had come in from New Jersey to see what was wrong. She said something about shallow breathing. There were some words to the effect of calling a private ambulance service, of Brian being too weak to move from his bedroom to the elevator, then the intensive care unit, some diagnosis of atypical pneumonia, some negative HIV test, some reversal of the pneumonia diagnosis, some rapid deterioration of lung tissue, doctors "in a quandary," relatives flying up from Florida. Apparently there was a priest involved; things were that bad. Brian's mother spoke in simple, even words. I debated in my mind whether I should call her Mrs. Peterson or Jan, her first name. If I called her Mrs. Peterson, as I probably had in the past, would that mean that things were normal, that I was acting "normal" about it? She told me not to come to the hospital, that Brian didn't want people to see him as he looked very bad. I wrote a card and sent it by messenger from my office the next day. I had one of those jobs which allowed for such things. I worked at a magazine about beauty. I had an office and a computer and a phone with many lines. I had swank health insurance, a gym membership, all the things Brian never got around to acquiring because he never got off the frozen plateau I'd long considered to be nothing more than his pathetic ass.

This is about death. Although for Brian, death seemed to be there from the beginning. It seemed to have settled, seed-like, into his pores from the time he was small. For Brian, there was something about life that he just couldn't do. And what was amazing was the unusual way in which he chose not to do it. Nothing about him was morbid. His world was clean and high in quality. He took hour-long showers. He wore Armani jackets. He drove his very expensive car to New Orleans for the hell of it. He dropped out of two colleges because he wasn't enjoying them. He refused to get a job because he didn't want one. His parents paid his rent on a huge apartment in SoHo, which he decorated with the obvious accessories of one who sees life through fashion magazines and Williams-Sonoma catalogs. On the walls, he had the Ansel Adams photograph, the Van Gogh print. Brian was the owner of six separate remote controls. There was the television, the VCR, the cassette player, the compact disc player, the other cassette player, the cable box. As with his magazines, he often spread the remote controls out into a fan-like shape on the chrome coffee table. He dusted and vacuumed every day. He talked about his life as being "very good."

Brian was a firm believer in not spending time doing anything that wasn't enjoyable. The result is that he did very little; there was never much to enjoy. I say this as a person who only really knew him from the beginning of adolescence to the end of it, a time when pleasure comes in tiny spurts, when happiness presents itself in bursts at the ends of long, painful confusion. He had absolutely no concept of work, of the notion of reward following sacrifice, of dark preceding dawn and all of that. It seems unlikely that he really ever knew how to study, that he understood what it meant to make a phone call in order to find a job or make a professional connection or even arrange for anything other than Chinese food delivery or a haircut, the latter of which he obtained at Bergdorf Goodman's for eighty-five dollars. I have never in my life witnessed a person like Brian, a person who never witnessed life. I have never in my life allowed a person to cater to my whims the way he did, believing, as he did, that I had a life, albeit a cheap and filthy life, full of low-paying jobs, too much homework, and a college dorm room that smelled—as he declared the one time he visited—like "urine." Maybe this is what I liked about him, that he could so easily turn me into a working-class heroine, that even in my saddest moments of friendlessness and direc-tionlessness, I had ten times the life that he had. And I never even had to feel guilty; he still thought his life was great, an empty space of leisure and blank pleasure that I too could obtain if I had fewer of what he termed "hang-ups."

This is about death and it is about blame. I blame Brian's parents for everything. The thing I say to no one is that they killed him. By paying his rent, by not making him study trigonometry or stay in college, by not saying no to the car or the apartment, or the gas money for solitary trips to nowhere, or the racks and racks of Paul Stewart shirts, Howard and Jan Peterson caused the death of their son.

The moment I declared this in my mind is the moment I became despicable. The emotions that surround my experience of Brian's death are by far the ugliest and most unforgiving sentiments I have bestowed on any event of my life. I chose, perhaps for my own sanity, more likely because I was too afraid to choose anything else, to feel as if his death at twenty-two had been imminent from the day he was born. Because Brian died of no defined cause, because the diagnosis was inconclusive, because his parents allowed no autopsy, because he simply *died*, I chose to believe it happened on purpose. I chose to feel as if death for him was an achievement, a blessing, a trophy honoring all that he never bothered to complete. I chose to take his death as a cautionary tale, a message that, if one did not *do*, one would die. So I did quite a bit. I worked long hours. I swam at 5:30 in the morning. I told myself that I was going places, that I was a "comer." Brian, of course, was a "goner." Like the unearned Armani jackets, death became him. The turns of phrase went on and on.

Brian's death took less than three weeks to complete. He was in the hospital for seventeen days. The day he went in was the day most of our mutual friends from childhood had flown back from Christmas vacation to the homes that were constituting the early part of their adulthoods. This meant California, Ohio, Massachusetts. I lived directly across the park from Mount Sinai Hospital, where Brian lay bloated from virus-fighting steroids and motionless from paralytic drugs. Any movement, the doctors said, would have stressed his lungs. When he lost consciousness, his parents asked me to start coming over; they believed he'd hear my voice and "wake up." I took the bus to the hospital every third night. This was what I had promised myself: That even though his father called me twice a day to give me a "report"—"They still don't know;" "Things are better;" "No, they're worse;" "The numbers on the machine are up today;" "I was thinking about that time on Nantucket, did Brian ever mention it?"—I would not wreck my life by living, as they did, in the visitors' lounge of the Intensive Care Unit on the fourth floor of the Guggenheim Pavilion.

This is also about lying.

The Peterson family unit was a tiny thing—mom, dad, kid. There were no other siblings, only a handful of relatives. No neighbors. No friends. I believe Howard Peterson received a visit at the hospital from his boss. After a few trips to the fourth-floor lounge, after a few times of seeing these parents who couldn't speak, who couldn't bathe, who had lost all sense of time, after a few times of seeing the faces of the nurses and medical students and even the relatives of patients who had been merely shot in the cranium or shattered on motorcycles, I realized that the only way to handle the situation was to tell lies. Though it was plain that death was something already occurring, that this hospital stay was no longer about healing but about the slow submergence of a doomed ocean liner, the game to play seemed to be a game of denial. Jan and Howard Peterson were interested in everything that was not reality. They were interested in all that their son was not. They wanted to know about his friends and what movies he liked and, as they put it, "his art." They wanted to know who had left the pack of Lucky Strikes on his kitchen table and should that person be called regarding "the situation."

I told them yes and yes and yes. I scrounged for morsels of truth and expanded them into benign, purposeful lies. I told them Brian liked Fellini—it was true, I believed, that he had once rented *8 1/2* from the video store. I told them he was devoted to his writing, that he planned to arrive at a masterpiece one day and buy them a house in Nantucket. To their delight, I spoke about him in the present tense. I pontificated about all that I planned to do with him when he, as they kept putting it, "got out." I surmised that Brian would someday write a lovely prose poem about his stay in the hospital. They ate this up, "more, more" they said without speaking, though Howard spoke a lot, "needed to keep talking," he said, whereas his wife lay on the plastic couch in the lounge and looked at the ceiling.

I came to know Howard Peterson better than I'd ever known a friend's parent. Though I hated him for the delusional, sugar-coated approach he had taken to parenting, and obsessed as I was at the time with what I defined as *reality*, with the cold, hard truths of the corporate working-world, and rent-paying, and late-night subway rides taken because a cab would cost too much, I wasn't outwardly cruel enough to express any inkling of opinion. I hated him for denying his son the postmodern rites of passage, for never arguing with Brian, for never hesitating to write the checks, for perpetually neglecting to crack the whip. Even now, it is a mystery to me who Jan and Howard Peterson are. For twenty years they lived in a small and badly decorated house in New Jersey. They drove a 1983 Oldsmobile Cutlass. Howard worked as a bond trader. Jan did nothing. They became rich in the 1980s and spent it all on Brian, invested it all in the enterprise that seemed an experiment in passivity, as if lack of movement was the ultimate freedom, as if people who say "I'm going to win the lottery and spend the rest of my life doing nothing" really know what they're talking about.

But my relationship to Howard during these days in the visitors' lounge presented me with an interesting set of rules, a subtle opportunity for mind manipulation. Since Jan wouldn't speak, and talking to Howard terrified me in that he broke down in tears after just a few sentences, my decision to "think positively" about the situation, to be optimistic and cheerful and phrase things in precisely the opposite way than I normally do, served the function of putting myself at a remove from the whole thing. As actors say, I made a choice. I made a decision to cross to upstage left, to tell them that Brian was working on a screenplay, to refrain from getting upset because, as I said, "There's nothing to be upset about because he's going to pull through." My best line was this: "Brian will not die because people our age can't conceive of death in relation to ourselves. It's not in his vocabulary, therefore it's impossible."

It was for this sort of language that Howard called me one night to come visit him in his hotel room. He and Jan were staying a few blocks from the hospital at a place called the Hotel Wales. Howard said he wanted to talk about Brian. He said he "wanted to gain greater insight" into his son. I was sitting in my room drinking wine from a plastic tumbler when he called. My bedroom window was open, and flecks of snow were floating in. A news report emitted from the clock radio, something about George Bush, who was technically still in office, although the inauguration was days away. I had been engrossed in the election, smitten by James Carville, newly invigorated by politics—the campaign buses and falling-down balloons of it all. Brian had taken little interest, though he'd appeared bemused by my chattering.

So this is what it was when Howard called: the wine in the tumbler, me still in my work clothes. I took a cab to the hotel and readied myself for more lies, for more of the acting I hadn't done since a high school performance of *The Man Who Came to Dinner*—a performance for which Brian had brought me flowers. I was terrified to meet Howard the way I had feared going onstage, the dread of the audience mixing with a longing for the whole thing to end in triumph, for some crowd to cheer, for a late-night cast party followed by peaceful sleep in my childhood bed.

This was a luxurious hotel, green and gold wallpaper, wood moldings polished until they were mirror-like. When Howard opened the door, he was wearing the same sweater he'd worn the past four times I'd seen him, only now there was a food stain on it. His hair stuck out on either side like a clown's. He wanted to hear the line again, the line about death not being in Brian's vocabulary. He wanted it repeated over and over, like a child hearing a bedtime story. I was afraid that if I flubbed the word order he'd correct me, that if I slipped into past tense he'd ask why. He said I was his favorite person to talk to these days, that the doctors were "paid to be pessimistic," that relatives were evasive, that his wife had given up and was simply praying.

The room was not a room but a suite—living room, bedroom, kitchen. Howard made himself a glass of water, took some pills out of his pocket, and swallowed them. He asked what books Brian read, what programs he watched on television. I said Dostoyevsky, Doctorow and

Seinfeld. I said *The Picture of Dorian Gray*; that one, I believed, was true. I said that Brian was a lover of the good life, that unlike the rest of us, he lived for the day, that he'd quit school because he'd realized it wasn't right for him. I and the rest of Brian's friends, I explained, were just robots for doing our homework, for not trying to beat the system. Brian was a rebel. He was a lover, a fighter, and a hero all in one. He would never die. There was no way it could happen.

This went on for three hours, until Howard went into the bedroom, lay down, and fell asleep. I waited ten minutes and slinked out. He'd left cab money for me on the table, which I took, like a whore. This was four days before the end.

Brian died around 6:30 in the morning, the time when I usually returned from my swim at the health club, my participation in the society in which Brian refused to take part. I arrived home, saw the light blinking on my answering machine, and knew. For a few minutes I avoided replaying the tape because there seemed no reason. Outside it was still dark, still dead, cold January. My chlorinated hair was frozen on my scalp because I never wore a hat to walk the four blocks from the club. Howard's voice was steady on the machine; "Are you there? Are you screening your calls? . . . Brian didn't make it." He began to say something else but his voice cracked and he hung up. All I could think was that I wouldn't have to go to the hospital anymore. All I could wonder was whether I should go to work. I had no inclination to cry, although I believe I tried, conjuring up sad stories, again like the high school actress to which this event had partially restored me. I tried to do something appropriate. I made coffee. I took a shower. I turned on the television and watched the news. It was inauguration day. Bush's out, Clinton's in.

The two families passed each other on the White House steps like baseball teams shaking hands after a game. Such somber, upright civility.

I had found my metaphor. I had found the moment upon which to seize, the symbol around which to fashion the circumstance of my friend's death. No longer a random occurrence, an inexplicable meeting with a bizarre virus no one else catches, Brian's death became for me a national mandate, an obligatory component of a cultural changing of the guard. Just as I had delighted in the fact that the Clinton campaign's theme song was Fleetwood Mac's "Don't Stop," a message that had prompted me to propel my thoughts vehemently into all that the future would bring—the information superhighway, congressional term limits, corporate-subsidized health clubs for hard-working, *realistic* people like me—I rationalized that Brian's refusal to ever think about tomorrow had lead to his demise. For the first time since he had become ill three weeks before, I allowed myself to spell the words out: Brian died because he refused to live. He refused to live because he refused to work. It was all out of some Ayn Rand manifesto: One must make profound sacrifices in order to live a life without compromise. Brian had attempted the latter without the former. He had seized the day so intensely that the day finally seized him. More turns of phrase. I reveled in them. I reclined back and watched my stylistic light show, curled up into my big, derisive comfy chair. In my mind, in the milieu that I had built around this event—the perfunctory hospital visits, the heading for the wine bottle the minute I returned home, the reluctance to tell other friends for fear that it would be awkward—I had set up an incident that had more to do with psychology than medicine. Brian was so drugged up, we were told, that he had no idea what was happening. He was a minor player. There was no dying involved, only the dealing with it. There was no body, only

Hallmark cards. No last breaths of life, but instead cigarettes in the breezeway outside the Guggenheim Pavilion. As far as I was concerned at the time, there would be no grief, only irony.

And the sickest part about the whole thing is that I felt the irony while it was actually going on. There was nothing retrospective about this view, no longing for hindsight, as it seemed to have emerged precociously while events were still occurring. The monstrosity that Brian's parents were being asked to wrap their minds around was more, I knew, than I could ever conceive of. The singular event of their dying son carried more horror than the worst catastrophes in the combined lives of myself and everyone I knew. What could I possibly have compared it to? Being rejected by Yale? That my milk-fed existence was now being soured by a tragedy that was not my own but someone else's put me in the peculiar position of grieving vicariously, a condition so cynical that the only option was to shut up about it. So I faked it. I threw myself into their needs with a duplicity intense enough to distract me from whatever sadness it did not occur to me to feel for myself.

Gamesmanship is something this is also about. Verbal gamesmanship, *sparring*—though the feeling was more like hitting a tennis ball against a wall.

The words I said to Jan and Howard Peterson after their son was dead were even bigger lies than the ones I'd said when he wasn't. I continued with the present tense. "Brian's probably laughing at us now." And "Brian, though he is sad to leave you, is probably fascinated by whatever he is experiencing now." They loved this—especially Howard, who in the forty-eight hours between inauguration day and the funeral, had become obsessed with the afterlife, "the other side," as he called it. I spoke at the mass. I regarded this as an opportunity to do some writing, to "be creative," which was something my job was not allowing. I was a huge hit: People came up to me at the burial and congratulated me on my performance. My parents, though disconcerted at my use of the present tense in my speech, remarked that I was a skilled speaker. For me and the few friends who had returned home for the funeral, seeing our parents was almost worse than seeing Jan and Howard. They wore on their faces the look of having just avoided a fatal car crash. They were like people run off the road, shell-shocked drivers, breathing heavily and staring at the steering wheel while the tractor trailer ambled on ahead. "All I can think is thank God it's them and not us," my mother said to me out loud. I hadn't worn a coat—I didn't own a proper one to wear with a dress—and someone else's mother went home between the mass and the burial to fetch me one, which she angrily insisted I wear as we stood by the grave. My father expressed his fear that I would catch Brian's mysterious virus. Like me, he wanted to know the mechanics of the thing, how and where it gained its entry, what Brian had done to contract it, what error in judgment had been made to cause this.

After the burial, I returned to my apartment in the city, threw up, and continued on with my life. I came to see grief as something I would simply never have. I perceived it as a sentiment that dwelled in the hearts of others, tucked neatly underneath a rug I'd never even owned. I became obsessed with movement, with productivity. At the time, this meant doing a good job at work, being the best editorial assistant a slick beauty magazine ever had. I wrote killer photo captions, answered my phone perkily, filled out invoices until eight o'clock at night. I did all the things Brian never did. I didn't mention "the situation" to anyone. My parents called to check on me, thrilled when I didn't mention the event, relieved when I seemed not to have a cold.

After about three months, Howard called and asked if I wanted to have dinner. He left a message on my machine, leaving Brian's old number as the place to call back. When I did, Brian's voice came on, deep and reticent. "I'm not available, please leave a message." I hated Howard all over again. He picked up when I spoke. He and Jan wanted to have dinner with me "in order to talk about Brian." They wanted me to meet them at Brian's apartment where they were staying. They wanted only to eat in restaurants where Brian had eaten, so could I recommend one?

Brian had only eaten in stylish places with ceiling fans and aspiring models at the bar. I had always hated this about him. I had always been embarrassed to go to establishments I had no business patronizing—establishments Brian had even less business eating in, although he always paid for both of us and ordered many drinks and an expensive entree and usually dessert. Once, while I was in college, he'd taken me to a place he'd read about in a magazine, a small club that had recently opened in SoHo. There we saw a girl from my school, a very rich girl with a famous mother, both of whom had been profiled in *Vanity Fair* a year earlier. This girl, who had never spoken to me on campus, came to our table and kissed me on the cheek. Brian was ecstatic. I was furious. I felt I was dressed terribly—and even if I had been dressed well, I would have been merely posing as a poseur, which was worse than merely existing in a state of delusion, which is what Brian did adamantly, with stubborn, insistent braggadocio. Still, this encounter held him for several weeks. He mentioned it repeatedly, talking about "Meghan's friend Countess X" to whichever of our other friends managed to drag themselves back into town to see him.

Restricting my lies to the big ones—how bad would it have been, after all, to suggest to Brian's parents that we eat at Pizzeria Uno because

Brian had loved the single deep dish?—I told Howard to make a reservation at Odeon because Brian loved it and often used it as a location in his writing, which was true. When I arrived at Brian's apartment, the Lucky Strikes were still on the kitchen table along with the December 22 edition of the *New York Post*, the January issue of *Esquire,* and the copy of *TV Guide* cracked at the spine. "We haven't touched these," said Howard. He was wearing corduroy pants and a polyester sweater. Jan wore wide wales and an L.L. Bean blouse. We went to Odeon. I scanned the room for fear of Countess X. Howard said he only wanted to order dishes that Brian had ordered. I had no recollection but told him the salmon.

It was during this meal that Jan and Howard first began to demonstrate their expertise in "the other side." Howard had read several books on the subject and had brought with him a list of the titles so that I, too, could learn more about "Brian's new life." Howard had had dreams, he explained, where Brian spoke to him and elaborated on the fun he was having. They had been to a psychic on Long Island who claimed to see Brian amid a field of roses and flanked by two other people, an older man—"probably his grandfather," said Jan—and a pretty, young girl whose name began with M. "I thought for a moment that might be you," she said. "But then you're not dead."

Then Jan declared loudly that she was considering killing herself. "I know just how I'd do it," she said. What got to me about this was not that she said it but that she said it so loudly. I looked over at the next table at three impeccably dressed men whose eyes seemed to momentarily shift over to us. It seems bizarre to me now that I didn't ask her how she planned to kill herself for fear that it was an inappropriate question. It seems bizarre that even after this meal, after I turned down their invitation to go to a late movie, after I again took cab fare from them, which I pocketed and instead rode the subway, I met Jan and Howard several more times. This went on for about a year. Howard would call every few months, and if I was in a guilty mood, which I almost always was, flagellating myself as I did about every inadequate job performance or overdue phone bill or call I screened for fear it would be them, I said yes. I said yes and continued to lie and say that I had read the afterlife books and that I, too, awaited the day of my death so I could see Brian again and that the world was hardly worth inhabiting when such a vibrant figure was removed from it.

The dynamic was this: The more I saw Jan and Howard, the more evil thoughts I harbored, which caused me guilt, which caused me to dig in my heels and see them again. This was my self-styled redemption, my faux little journey into good Samaritanism. If I saw the Petersons on a Saturday, I could be bad for the rest of the week. If I lied to Howard about the salmon, I could call a co-worker a bitch behind her back on Monday. What happened was that I began to hate the world. Just as I hated Jan and Howard for being so lax as parents that their son died of what I believed to be inertia, I hated everyone else for existing in a condition that I defined as "fake." Like Holden Caulfield, I became obsessed with "phoniness." I saw everyone as innate liars, as zombified self-deluders who were dangers to themselves as well as the rest of the world. I hated people who walked too slowly down the sidewalk, grocery store clerks who took too long to count the change, days when there was nothing but junk mail. I hated anything that impeded whatever I considered to be progress, whatever I had determined was my ticket to a socialized, productive life. Unlike Brian, I would pursue a career. Unlike him, I would shop at the grocery store efficiently. I would meet friends for lunch and drinks and have people over to my apartment to watch the Oscars. I would walk quickly down the street because I actually had someplace to go. I would do anything necessary to participate in what I considered to be life, which, to me, meant getting up extremely early and doing things like putting all the apartment's trash into a small plastic bag, which I would throw out on the way to the club to go swimming, after which I would go to work, and for lunch go to the gourmet deli on Forty-sixth Street, where I would tap my fingers on the counter if the people in front of me were taking too long to order, because *I had somewhere to be*, because I was impressively busy with this thing called life, because I was sternly committed to the pursuit of whatever was the opposite of death.

By the following Christmas, Jan and Howard had stopped calling me. I had expected to hear from them around the anniversary of Brian's death, the one-year mark of the Clinton administration. When they didn't call I imagined them dead in their poorly decorated house. I imagined empty sleeping pill bottles on the night table, or a hose hooked up to the back of the Oldsmobile with Howard's lifeless body five feet away. Since I'd never learned how they planned to kill themselves, it was difficult to put my finger on one particular scenario. Like "the situation" itself, there seemed so many variations on the truth, so many evil interpretations of events upon which to fixate. Through one of our mutual friends, I learned they hadn't killed themselves. Like a normal person, this friend, in town for Christmas, had called Jan and Howard himself and then driven over to the house. Like a good person, he sat in the living room and spoke honestly about this horrible thing that had happened. Unlike me, he saw no reason to lie. Unlike me, he wasn't hung up on some twisted symbolism, on some mean-spirited rationalization employed to keep fear at bay, to keep grief a thing depicted in movies rather than a loss felt in one's own flesh.

Here's another true scene from the movie. It's a flashback, a time I remember with Brian from when we were small, playing with other kids. We stood in a circle and called off our teams, the reds versus the blues, something like that. Then we needed an "it," a dreaded tagger who would tap us on the shoulder and freeze us. No one wanted the job, including myself, and I'd watched as Brian just stood there, silent amid the chants, bewildered as the shouting came over him. "Not it!" I yelled. "Not it!" someone else yelled. "Not it!" we all said until there was no one but Brian, a pale and clueless eight-year-old, suspended in those moments before realizing he'd lost the game. And so it was him. He was it.

Acknowledgments

These essays arose from my good fortune of being in the wrong places at the right times just as often as I've stumbled into the right places at the right times. I am indebted to a number of wise people who have shown me the value of not always knowing wrong from right. Thanks to Michael Scammell, for noticing; Joshua Sessions, for reading (and reading and reading); Sarah Wolf, Emilie Dyer, Sara Eckel and Alison Schecterfor talking and listening (and reading); and Sloan Harris, for waiting.

Thomas Beller was one of my earliest champions. He's one of the rare people whose taste fuels his energy rather than depletes it and I'm privileged to be a beneficiary of his chutzpah and goodwill. I am grateful to Robert Bingham, Daniel Pinchbeck, and all of the editors of Open City, especially to Joanna Yas, who doesn't let her ability to actually get things done detract from her imagination, foresight, and talent.

The ultimate thanks goes to my parents; Glen Daum, who taught me, through music, everything I know about writing a sentence; and Rachael Daum, who passed along the drive to get those sentences read.

Also available from **OPEN CITY** . . .

OPEN CITY Magazine

"An athletic balance of hipster glamour and highbrow esoterica."
—*The Village Voice*

actual air by David Berman

"One of the funniest, smartest, and sweetest books of the year."
—*GQ*

Venus Drive by Sam Lipsyte

"A wickedly gifted writer."
—Robert Stone

....

Send checks or money orders payable to: Open City, Inc., 225 Lafayette Street, Suite 1114, New York, NY 10012. For credit card orders, see www.opencity.org.

☐ Actual Air by David Berman $12.95   ☐ Venus Drive by Sam Lipsyte $13.00
☐ Open City four-issue subscription $32.00

Name: _____

Address: _____

City: _____ State: _____ Zip: _____

Foreign Postage per item/four issues: Canada
and Mexico: $1/$4; Elsewhere:$5/$20.